"This volume offers a timely set of papers on the origins and future trajectories of the South China Sea disputes. It will be useful to both scholars and policymakers alike who are attempting to grapple with the rise of China and its consequences for the United States and the regional states."

Professor T.V. Paul, McGill University, Canada

"The volume so ably elucidates some of the most confounding and contentious policies and postures unfolding the U.S.–China rivalry in and around the South China Sea. By foregrounding contemporary geopolitics in various historical, technical, legalistic elements of this rivalry in the larger canvas of rapidly changing global politics, this volume not just stands out in highlighting system-shaping capabilities of this rivalry but also alludes to its likely future trajectories."

Professor Swaran Singh, Jawaharlal Nehru University, India

"This book provides a detailed overview of the South China Sea dispute and its importance to questions of territory, foreign policy, nationalism, and economics. The contributions each provide are thorough research and analysis. The book should be of interest to both academics and those in the policy community. A great read!"

Professor Amanda Murdie, University of Georgia, U.S.A.

"The South China Sea is certain to remain a major epicenter of geopolitical conflict. China's claims to almost all of the SCS threaten Southeast Asian states' free navigation, and exploitation of rich fishing and mineral resources. Beijing's militarization of "artificial" islands, Belt and Road strategy, and growing pressure on Hong Kong and Taiwan heighten tensions. The stage is set for U.S.–China confrontations and escalating violence. Roy's *Navigating Uncertainty* offers first-rate essays on all the issues, written by experts in accessible language, and should have great appeal to specialists, students, policymakers, and general readers. Highly recommended."

Professor Yale H. Ferguson, Rutgers University, U.S.A.

"China's growing power projection in the energy-rich South China Sea has been a source of serious concern to the major stakeholders in the region, especially the United States and ASEAN member states. A battery of scholars have critically illuminated multiple implications of the South China Sea conflict and suggested pragmatic measures to defuse the tension. This edited volume makes an important contribution to the understanding of conflicting interests of regional actors from the geopolitical and geoeconomic perspective. It is highly recommended as an essential read for policymakers, the strategic community, academia, and graduate students."

Professor B.M. Jain,
Editor-in-Chief, *Indian Journal of Asian Affairs*, India

"Nalanda Roy has once again taken a holistic approach to one of the most important issues in East Asia. Giving the reader a wide variety of assessments and assertions, providing insights that have rarely been addressed, and writing in clear language that allows students and scholars alike to absorb the scholarship are all aspects of this work that will make it important for studying geopolitical issues in East Asia. This work will be important reading for those who have an interest in the South China Sea, as well as those who want to understand security issues in the Asia-Pacific region."

Professor Bruce Bechtol, Angelo State University, U.S.A.

"The South China Sea is one of the most heavily traversed and hotspot waterways, as a corollary of which, the overlapping territorial disputes and intransigence of an aggressive China have propelled the littorals as a high priority region in the dynamics of Asia-Pacific security. China's aggressive claims to the nine-dash area have erected a new "Great Wall" at Sea. Given this tumultuous backdrop, the chapters of this book are well written, lucid, and engaging. The authors of this book offer thoughtful insights and perceptive strategic analyses of the complexities of this issue. This book reflects itself as an extraordinarily illuminating text for readers who want to graft the principal ideas and events surrounding this never-ending geopolitical saga."

Professor Tridib Chakraborti, Jadavpur University, India

Navigating Uncertainty in the SOUTH CHINA SEA DISPUTES

INTERDISCIPLINARY PERSPECTIVES

Navigating Uncertainty in the SOUTH CHINA SEA DISPUTES

INTERDISCIPLINARY PERSPECTIVES

EDITOR

NALANDA ROY

(Georgia Southern University, USA)

World Scientific

NEW JERSEY • LONDON • SINGAPORE • BEIJING • SHANGHAI • HONG KONG • TAIPEI • CHENNAI • TOKYO

Published by

World Scientific Publishing Europe Ltd.
57 Shelton Street, Covent Garden, London WC2H 9HE
Head office: 5 Toh Tuck Link, Singapore 596224
USA office: 27 Warren Street, Suite 401-402, Hackensack, NJ 07601

Library of Congress Cataloging-in-Publication Data
Names: Roy, Nalanda, editor.
Title: Navigating uncertainty in the South China Sea disputes : interdisciplinary perspectives / Nalanda Roy, Georgia Southern University, USA.
Description: London ; Hackensack, NJ : World Scientific, [2021] | Includes bibliographical references and index.
Identifiers: LCCN 2020032979 | ISBN 9781786349279 (hardcover) | ISBN 9781786349286 (ebook) | ISBN 9781786349293 (ebook other)
Subjects: LCSH: South China Sea--International status. | Maritime boundaries--South China Sea. | Marine resources development--Law and legislation--South China Sea. | South China Sea--Economic conditions.
Classification: LCC KZ1692 .N38 2021 | DDC 341.4/480916472--dc23
LC record available at https://lccn.loc.gov/2020032979

British Library Cataloguing-in-Publication Data
A catalogue record for this book is available from the British Library.

For any available supplementary material, please visit
https://www.worldscientific.com/worldscibooks/10.1142/Q0272#t=suppl

Desk Editors: Balamurugan Rajendran/Michael Beale/Shi Ying Koe

Typeset by Stallion Press
Email: enquiries@stallionpress.com

https://doi.org/10.1142/9781786349286_fmatter

Foreword

The South China Sea has quickly emerged to be a major hot spot in international politics today due to its strategic location, natural resources, and overlapping claims by several states. Most notably it has become a venue for U.S.–China rivalry, which makes the area potentially explosive.

At its core, the South China Sea issue reflects the changing landscape of international political economy. The twin developments after the 1990s — large explorations of oil and natural gas and the rapid rise of China — fundamentally changed the dynamics of political economy in the Asia-Pacific region. Controversies in the South China Sea are not just about territories and resources, they also concern prestige of the states involved and the new international order, in which China and the United States are competing for primacy.

For decades, the United States has been the dominant power in Asia, providing security — and deterrence — in a region full of historical and territorial disputes. The focus of countries surrounding the South China Sea has been to promote economic growth and to catch up with their more advanced neighbors such as Japan and Australia. In fact, many of these countries followed the "developmental state" model first practiced in Japan. Many of them also became manufacturing and exporting powerhouses. Peace and prosperity continue to be the common interests of all these countries.

China's rise has created both opportunities and worries. Its sweeping claims over the South China Sea based on its historical records have faced stiff challenges. The statement that the area has been part of China "since ancient times" is not convincing to other claimants. China has not clearly defined its maritime boundaries despite the existence of the vague "Nine-Dash Line." As China's power continues to grow, some people worry that China may turn the South China Sea into an exclusive Chinese lake.

Growing nationalism at home makes it difficult for China to appear weak in foreign affairs. China has adopted the so-called "wolf warrior" diplomacy in recent years as a result of its growing confidence and the leadership's promotion of "a fighting spirit." China is unlikely to make concessions in the South China Sea under the current circumstances.

Countries in the South China Sea area are highly interdependent. China has exercised economic statecraft to achieve its geostrategic goals. While strengthening its presence in the South China Sea, China has provided economic enticements to other claimants, which often puts these states in a dilemma about whether they should confront or cooperate with China. The Philippines is a case in point. In January 2013, the Philippine government formally initiated arbitration proceedings against China's claim in the South China Sea. On July 12, 2016, the Permanent Court of Arbitration backed the Philippines, saying that there was no evidence that China had historically exercised exclusive control over the waters or resources, hence there was "no legal basis for China to claim historic rights" over the area. China did not participate in the arbitration and rejected the ruling, calling it "ill-founded." President Rodrigo Duterte who came to power right before the ruling has downplayed the dispute and emphasized cooperation with China as a key interest of his country. The Philippines has joined China's Belt and Road Initiative and has benefited from trade and infrastructure cooperation with China.

The involvement of external powers has made the dispute more complex. The United States has insisted that the South China Sea is international space where it can operate "freedom of navigation" missions. To counter China's island-building activities, the United States, often joined by its allies such as Japan and Australia, has conducted military exercises in the region.

"Freedom of navigation" is a common interest of all, including China. Security of this busy commercial waterway is critical to many countries. However, China suspects that the United States is using "freedom of navigation" as a pretext to counter China's growing influence and block China's power projection. China has been aggressively expanding its fleet of oceangoing warships, increasing its stock of hypersonic "carrier killer" cruise missiles, and improving its undersea technology. All of this gives it more confidence not only in responding to U.S. patrols but also raises the stakes for a potential conflict.

Most countries in Asia welcome America's continued presence, but China is right next door. Will the United States make room for China's development? Can the United States and China live peacefully? The last thing Asian countries want is to be forced to choose between the two great powers.

As Singaporean Prime Minister Lee Hsien Loong remarked, both the United States and China face fundamental choices. The United States must decide whether to view China's rise as an existential threat and try to hold China back through all available means or to accept China as a major power in its own right. For its part, China must decide whether to try to get its way as an unencumbered major power, prevailing by dint of its sheer weight and economic strength — but at the risk of strong push-back, not just from the United States but from other countries too.[a]

Asian countries have so far enjoyed the best of both worlds, building economic relationships with China while maintaining strong ties with the United States. However, growing competition between the two powers has made such a tranquil way of life increasingly difficult to keep. Whether the twin objectives of peace and prosperity will be achieved in the future largely depends on how countries in the region manage their differences and focus on areas where they can cooperate. A code of conduct must be reached and abided by, which should emphasize peaceful resolution of disputes and resource-sharing by claimants while maintaining freedom of navigation for all.

This concise book edited by Professor Nalanda Roy does a fine job in highlighting some of the complex issues and perspectives related to the South China Sea. It will help readers understand why the South China Sea is so important to countries in the Asia-Pacific, how it affects the global community, and what can be done moving forward.

Zhiqun Zhu
Lewisburg, Pennsylvania
July 2020

[a]Lee Hsien Loong, "The Endangered Asian Century: America, China, and the Perils of Confrontation," *Foreign Affairs*, June 4, 2020. https://www.foreignaffairs.com/articles/asia/2020-06-04/lee-hsien-loong-endangered-asian-century.

https://doi.org/10.1142/9781786349286_fmatter

About the Editor

Nalanda Roy is an Associate Professor in the Department of Political Science and International Studies and an Inclusive Excellence Faculty Fellow at Georgia Southern University. Dr. Roy serves as a visiting scholar with the Center for Genocide and Human Rights, Rutgers University, and is the associate editor of the *Journal of Asian Security and International Affairs*, SAGE. She also serves as the board member for *International Studies Review*, Oxford University Press, *Perspectives on Global Development and Technology*, Brill Publications, *Journal of the Royal Society for Asian Affairs*, Routledge, and *South Asian Survey*, SAGE. She published her first book, *Bitter Moments — The Story of Indonesian Fragmentation*, in 2015. In 2016, she published *The South China Sea Disputes — Past, Present, and Future*. She also recently published *Exploring the Tripod: Immigration, Security, and Economy in the Post-9/11 United States* in 2020. Dr. Roy is on the board of directors with the City of Savannah and works for the Greater Savannah International Alliance.

https://doi.org/10.1142/9781786349286_fmatter

About the Contributors

Barry J. Balleck received a B.A. in political science and an M.A. in international studies from Brigham Young University. He received his Ph.D. in political science from the University of Colorado at Boulder with emphases in international relations, American politics, and political theory. Upon completion of his degree, Dr. Balleck joined the faculty of Georgia Southern University, where he held a joint appointment in both the Department of Political Science and the Center for International Studies. Dr. Balleck currently serves as the chair and department head of the Department of Political Science and International Studies at Georgia Southern University. For the past twenty-three years, he has also directed Georgia Southern University's Model United Nations (MUN) program, one of the oldest and most continuous programs of its kind in the country. Dr. Balleck has directed the Georgia Southern MUN delegation to several national awards and has conducted dozens of MUN conferences for middle- and high-school students from Georgia, South Carolina, Tennessee, and Florida.

Dr. Balleck has research and teaching interests in the fields of international and domestic terrorism, U.S. foreign policy, the rhetoric of politics, the United Nations, and international human rights. He has dozens of conference presentations to his credit and has published in journals such as *Presidential Studies Quarterly, Politics & Policy*, and *Peace Psychology Review*. Dr. Balleck has three recently-published books that all focus on the growing threat of political extremism in the United States. These books are: *Allegiance to Liberty: The Changing Face of Patriots, Militias, and Political Violence in America*, *Modern American Extremism and Domestic Terrorism: An Encyclopedia of Extremists and Extremist Groups*, and *Encyclopedia of Hate Groups in America*.

Romi Jain, Ph.D. is a postdoctoral research and teaching fellow at the University of British Columbia — Okanagan campus, British Columbia, Canada. She is the vice president of the *Indian Journal of Asian Affairs* and has served as editor-in-chief of *Harvard Asia Quarterly*, a publication of the Harvard University Asia Center. She has published many articles on China's economic development, trade, and political economy in peer-reviewed international journals such as *Asian Affairs: An American Review*, *Journal of Third World Studies*, and *American Journal of Chinese Studies*. Her special article is forthcoming in *Economic and Political Weekly*, India's premium academic journal. Jain's articles and commentaries have appeared in newspapers and magazines such as *Asia Times, The Diplomat*, and *Eurasia Review*.

Daniel H. Katz, Ph.D. is a nonresident scholar for the Baker Institute China Studies Program and a senior geopolitical risk analyst for a global company. Katz's current research focuses on defense diplomacy and is the subject of a forthcoming book.

Katz previously worked at the U.S. Department of State, the Center for a New American Security, and the International Institute for Strategic Studies, Asia. He has written extensively on global security issues and U.S.–China relations. Katz is proficient in Mandarin Chinese. He holds a Ph.D. in strategic studies from the S. Rajaratnam School of International Studies at Nanyang Technological University, a double master of science degree in international affairs from Peking University and the London School of Economics, and a B.A. in international studies and classics (Latin) from Yale University. His publications are listed at https://www.bakerinstitute.org/experts/daniel-h-katz/.

Christopher B. Primiano is a part time lecturer in the Department of Political Science at Hunter College. Chris' research focuses on Chinese domestic and international politics. His articles have appeared in *Journal of Chinese Political Science*, *Peace Economics, Peace Science and Public Policy*, *East Asia*, *Asia Pacific Journal of Sport and Social Science*, *International Politics*, *China: An International Journal*, *China Report*, and *Journal of Muslim Minority Affairs*. He can be reached at cbprimiano@gmail.com.

David Rosenberg is a Visiting Fellow in the Department of Political and Social Change, Coral Bell School of Asia Pacific Affairs, Australian National University; Emeritus Professor of Political Science, Middlebury College, Vermont, U.S.A.; and Editor for www.southchinasea.org. His research focuses on resource management and maritime security in the South China Sea. His publications are listed at http://www.middlebury.edu/academics/ps/faculty/node/652187.

https://doi.org/10.1142/9781786349286_fmatter

Acknowledgments

It is my great pleasure to thank my family for their loving support and constant encouragement. I am also thankful to my graduate research assistant, Amber Brantley, for her editorial assistance with my book. Amber is pursuing a Master of Arts, with a focus in political science from Georgia Southern University. Sincere thanks as well to my graduate school mentor, Dr. Yale Ferguson, Rutgers University, for his continued interest in my work.

https://doi.org/10.1142/9781786349286_fmatter

Contents

https://doi.org/10.1142/9781786349286_fmatter

List of Figures and Table

https://doi.org/10.1142/9781786349286_fmatter

Acronyms

A2/AD	Anti-access/Area denial
AIIB	Asian Infrastructure Investment Bank
AMTI	Asia Maritime Transparency Initiative
ASEAN	Association of Southeast Asian Nations
BRI	Belt and Road Initiative
CCG	China Coast Guard
CCSBT	The Commission for the Conservation of Southern Bluefin Tuna
CLCS	United Nations Commission on the Limits of the Continental Shelf
COC	Code of Conduct
COVID-19	Corona Virus Disease-19
CPEC	China–Pakistan Economic Corridor
CPTPP	Comprehensive and Progressive Agreement for Trans-Pacific Partnership
CUES	Code for Unplanned Encounters at Sea
DOC	Declaration on the Conduct of Parties in the South China Sea
DOD	U.S. Department of Defense
ECS	East China Sea
EEZ	Exclusive Economic Zone
ETIM	East Turkestan Islamic Movement
EU	European Union
FONOP	Freedom of Navigation Operations
GDP	Gross Domestic Product

IEA	International Energy Agency
IOR	Indian Ocean Region
IR	International Relations
LNG	Liquefied Natural Gas
MCKIP	Malaysia–China Kuantan Industrial Park
MoU	Memorandum of Understanding
MSR	Marine Scientific Research
NATO	North Atlantic Treaty Organization
NGCP	National Grid Corporation of the Philippines
OBOR	One Belt One Road
OECD	Organization for Economic Co-operation and Development
PAFMM	People's Armed Forces Maritime Militia
PBGEA	Pilipino Banana Growers and Exporters Association
PLA	People's Liberation Army
PLAN	People's Liberation Army Navy
PRC	People's Republic of China
PSA	Philippine Statistics Authority
ReCAAP	The Regional Cooperation Agreement on Combating Piracy and Armed Robbery against Ships in Asia
ROC	Republic of China (Taiwan)
SAR	Search and Rescue
SCS	South China Sea
SEZs	Special Economic Zones
SLOCS	Sea Lanes of Communication
STRAITREP	Ship Traffic Management System in the Straits of Malacca and Singapore
TPP	Trans-Pacific Partnership
UN	United Nations
UNCLOS	United Nations Convention on the Law of the Sea
UNCTAD	United Nations Conference on Trade and Development
UUV	Unmanned Underwater Vehicle
WHO	World Health Organization
ZoPFFC	Zone of Peace, Freedom, Friendship, and Cooperation

https://doi.org/10.1142/9781786349286_0001

Chapter 1

Introduction

Nalanda Roy

Even the finest sword plunged into saltwater will eventually rust.

— Sun Tzu

1.1 Importance of the South China Sea

While the Coronavirus outbreak has become a pandemic and created a difficult challenge for China, her Asian neighbors, as well as for the entire world, the South China Sea is witnessing fresh stand-offs over energy exploration between countries like Indonesia, Malaysia, China, and Vietnam. Despite the pandemic, Beijing has not reduced her activities in the South China Sea; instead, the Chinese government's years-long assertiveness has intensified further. The South China Sea (hereafter SCS) has long been regarded as one of the most complex regional maritime systems in East Asia. The SCS is a semi-enclosed sea bordered by member countries of the Association of Southeast Asian Nations, including Brunei, Cambodia, Indonesia, Singapore, Malaysia, the Philippines, Thailand, and Vietnam, though not Laos and Myanmar. The SCS region is significant in terms of its geostrategic location, oil resources, and geoeconomic and marine biological diversity and has become important due to competition for overlapping claims to the sea and potential territorial disputes among the countries. Figure 1.1 shows the occupied islands by the claimants in the SCS.

Figure 1.1. The South China Sea

Source: South China Sea Virtual Library www.southchinasea.org.

One of the most difficult issues impacting upon sovereignty claims and disputes in the SCS is the "U-shaped line" or the "dotted" or "the nine-dotted line" that dates back to 1947. That year, Chiang Kai-shek defined China's claims by an area limited by nine dots covering most of the SCS. In 1951, this claim was formalized by Zhou Enlai. Opinions vary regarding the legality of this line in the SCS. The line explores a historical line of maritime rights over the disputed waters, and also puts forth arguments on China's so-called right to fishing and the right to explore in waters covered by the dotted line. Besides, the publication of China's new national map that incorporates either a 10th "dash" or even an "eleven dash" line has created ripples in Southeast Asia and beyond. Over time, it has become really difficult to connect Beijing's speculative dashes. The Asia Maritime Transparency Initiative (AMTI) warned that

> New energy development by Southeast Asian states anywhere within the nine-dash line will be met by persistent, high-risk intimidation from Chinese law enforcement and paramilitary vessels. [2]

Often referred to as "a dangerous, ongoing game of chicken," neighbors are challenging the dragon's claim of almost the entirety of the SCS through its so-called 9-dash line boundary. Neighbors are always skeptical when it comes to Beijing's history of power building in the region.

On several occasions, China has assured others that she would not use her military might and power to compel her neighbors; however, it has mostly been the opposite. China's unilateral move in claiming sovereignty over tiny atolls and islands are raising serious questions about the efficacy of international laws and norms pertaining to the territorial seas and continental shelf. For example, recently, China has been gathering Big Data for information superiority and pushing to control the digital infrastructure of other states. Besides, China's island reclamation activities together with its construction of military fortifications have heightened tensions among its neighbors, including the United States. Such activities would not only undermine China's bilateral relations with neighboring littoral states, such as Vietnam and the Philippines, but could lead to accidental escalation. As Sun Tzu stated:

> engage people with what they expect; it is what they are able to discern and confirms their projections. It settles them into predictable patterns of response, occupying their minds while you wait for the extraordinary moment — that which they cannot anticipate. [1]

1.1.1 *What lies beneath?*

The South China Sea is a semi-enclosed sea encompassing an area from the Karimata and Malacca Straits to the Strait of Taiwan, and it is around

3,500,000 square kilometers. It is bordered by member countries of the Association of Southeast Asian Nations (ASEAN), including Brunei, Cambodia, Indonesia, Singapore, Malaysia, the Philippines, Thailand, and Vietnam. With an increasing demand for, and competition over, natural resources in the region, it is often becoming difficult to maintain a balanced and humanistic approach within the global community. The SCS has numerous archipelagoes, islands, peninsulas, coral reefs, seasonally reversing monsoon winds, and underwater currents, which combine to produce favorable conditions for a fertile marine ecosystem. Before the 20th century, the South China Sea was of little interest to any of the potential claimants like China, Brunei, Malaysia, the Philippines, Thailand, and Vietnam. This region was not considered particularly dangerous; however, this has obviously changed since then due to the increasing demand for both tapped and untapped natural resources. Now, territorial sovereignty; disputed claims to islands, rocks, and reefs; jurisdiction over territorial waters; the region's strategic location; regional and international rights to use the seas for military purposes; maritime law and security; marine biological diversity; exclusive economic zones; rapid economic development; and environmental degradation have created a highly complex and dynamic international order in Asia.

The question is why do these disputes resonate so much? Why do they have far-reaching economic and geopolitical implications for Asia-Pacific nations and the rest of the world? This region is located along major routes used by crude oil tankers from the Persian Gulf and container ships transporting goods; it also has promising offshore oil and gas reserves. This edited volume will survey the region's strategic location, energy resources, geoeconomic importance, and marine biological diversity to analyze the significance of territorial disputes based on the overlapping claims of different countries. The contributors have explored the major security implications of the SCS disputes in the region and analyzed Beijing's effort to establish a maritime and continental zone of influence.

The study is designed to answer two key questions: first, why is the area of vital importance to Asia-Pacific nations? Second, what is its impact on the global community? Since all maritime traffic in the sea passes between the Spratly and Paracel Islands, their sovereignty and strategic control are crucial. Sea power is experiencing a major revival today. As Alfred Thayer Mahan [1890] pointed out, sea power consists of a navy and a fleet and requires places where the navy can be protected. The Spratly and Paracel Islands offer places to shelter and re-equip naval forces. China seems to be following its blue water navy strategy, both to increase its prestige and to expand its national interests. While China's admirals have decided to work more closely with neighboring countries, cooperating with the Japanese and Indian navies in patrolling against piracy off the coast of Somalia, this "go along to get along" policy is often criticized for being unrealistic. Experts hope that such cooperation will have a positive, normative effect on civilian and military leadership, but it may work differently in waters closer to China.

The four main island groups in the SCS are the Paracels, the Spratlys, the Pratas, and Macclesfield Bank. Before the end of the Cold War, Russian and U.S. Navy facilities in Vietnam and the Philippines largely stabilized power in the region. However, their withdrawal has made China the dominant naval force. Neighbors fear that Beijing is trying to establish the entire region as a Chinese lake. Sovereignty disputes have arisen mostly over two strategically important archipelagos, the Paracels and the Spratlys. The Paracels consist of fifteen islands, several sandbanks, and reefs whose ownership is contested by China, Taiwan, and Vietnam. Having ousted the South Vietnamese in 1974, China now occupies all of these features and has an airfield on Woody Island. The Spratlys are of strategic, maritime, and economic importance because they lie along the principal sea lanes of communication (SLOCs) for commercial ships in the Indian and Pacific Oceans — the Singapore, Sunda, and Lombok straits and the straits of Malacca. The Spratly seabed is thought to contain the greatest concentration of oil and gas reserves in the SCS.

As Asia's energy consumption grows with economic development, access to and control over these resources will weigh heavily on claimant perceptions of the contested areas' value. China's blue water navy strategy and her desire to prevent any threat to what it describes as "China's historical waters" raise the risk of future armed conflict. Since a Code of Conduct has not been negotiated successfully, SCS disputes are hard to resolve. Military skirmishes have occurred numerous times, and Chinese encroachment on Mischief Reef since 1995 has provoked actions by the Philippines. However, a severe crisis may be avoided because territorial issues involving natural resources have a higher probability of peaceful settlement on humanitarian grounds and to reap the benefits of resource sharing.

1.2 Organization

Navigating Uncertainty in the South China Sea Disputes: Interdisciplinary Perspectives will look at the issue of regional rivalries and how economic, political, and security interests within a regional context drive the foreign policies of aspiring regional and global hegemons. The organization of this edited volume is as follows: The Chapter 2 "China's Geoeconomic Diplomacy and the South China Sea Dispute: Promises and Pitfalls" critically examines China's geoeconomic diplomacy toward advancing its national interest *vis-à-vis* the SCS. The author critically examines how China is vigorously practicing economic statecraft in achieving its foreign policy goals with its growing economic clout. The chapter further describes China's hard power tools of coercion and inducement in dealing with Vietnam and the Philippines, which are among the parties to the SCS dispute. It assesses the strength of China's geoeconomic diplomacy and illustrates the areas of success and Beijing's promising moves. Finally, the chapter concludes by identifying the weak spots and challenges to geoeconomics.

The Chapter 3 "U.S.–China Rivalry and the Paradox of the South China Sea Disputes," includes a comparative historical analysis of security alliances in the post-WW2 Cold War period as well as the contemporary period involving the SCS. The study conducts a comparative survey of joint resource management programs currently in effect in East Asia. It also argues that the SCS disputes are widely seen to be driven by conflicting maritime boundary claims, increasing competition over maritime resources, and increasing nationalist pressure in domestic politics. The author explains that such conflicting claims persist because sovereignty claims based on historical grounds are widely disputed. International laws and rulings are often criticized for ambiguous terms and questionable assumptions. In addition to the disparate views among coastal countries about overlapping territorial claims, there are also conflicting views among coastal states and international stakeholders over national security and international freedom of navigation. Besides, intrinsically regional resources — such as fisheries — are vulnerable to over-exploitation and collapse.

The paradox is that these disputes are increasing among countries that otherwise have a high degree of cooperation on matters of trade and commerce. How can this paradox be resolved? China argues that the SCS has historically been Chinese, and it is only defending its territorial waters. It is increasing its naval and air activities in the vicinity and has created a series of artificial islands that could accommodate combat ships and aircraft, including air force bomber patrols. Chinese air force bombers have carried out a series of patrols over the South China Sea and have demonstrated a capability to go beyond the Cold War era line of containment or the "First Island Chain." China has sent its H-6K bombers to fly near the U.S. territory of Guam. Some Chinese military overflights have crossed Taiwan's Air Defense Identification Zone. The United States views South China Sea as an international waterway that allows "innocent passage" through its waters. The U.S. is increasing its "freedom of navigation" patrols there as well as military aid and joint naval exercises with coastal countries. The U.S. Defense Department now views China as a "strategic competitor" and a threat to U.S. power in the region. The Trump administration has started a "trade war" with China, claiming that "China is ripping off the U.S. on trade."

Is this the beginning of another Cold War? There are some similarities. Both China and the U.S. are now conducting increased air and sea patrols and exercises in the region to exhibit their strength, capacity, and preparedness. This rivalry puts pressure on countries around the SCS to take sides. Alliances and partnerships are being pursued to seek an advantage in the regional balance of power. However, there have not been any polarizing trends toward opposing forces like the post-war NATO (North Atlantic Treaty Organization) and Warsaw Pact military alliances. Despite the "war of words," neither side appears to seek armed conflict. However, as more combat ships and aircraft are added in a relatively small maritime space, the possibility of military encounters and/or accidents is increasing.

What can be done to improve resource sharing and maritime security in the South China Sea? There is ample precedent for cooperative resource management, as evidenced in the 2004 Sino-Vietnamese Tonkin Gulf agreements on boundary delimitation and joint fisheries management, CCSBT (the Commission for the Conservation of Southern Bluefin Tuna), STRAITREP (Ship Traffic Management System in the Straits of Malacca and Singapore), naval hotlines, anti-piracy programs, and numerous other bilateral and multilateral agreements. It is likely that in order to prevent acquiescence to China's claims over the Spratly Islands, the U.S., Japan, South Korea, India, Australia, and other like-minded countries should continue to urge China to define its maritime claims according to international maritime law. Their navies, either singly or jointly, should continue to assert traditional freedom of navigation by sailing through and flying over the

South China Sea where international law allows and either rebuff or ignore China's objections.

The Chapter 4 "China's Relations with the Philippines Since Duterte: Challenges and Opportunities" explores how in recent years, there has been ample attention devoted to China's actions in the SCS. In this chapter, the author explains why China's relations with the Philippines have improved since Rodrigo Duterte became president. In stark contrast to Benigno Aquino III, who was the previous leader of the Philippines, Duterte has embraced a very different position towards both China and the U.S., and this has resulted in a fundamental shift in China–Philippines relations. The chapter argues that China's relations with the Philippines should be examined in the larger political context of the SCS; hence, the role of the United States is also important to focus upon in accounting for why China's relations with the Philippines have improved. Finally, the chapter examines the broader implications of China–Philippines relationships in the SCS imbroglio.

The Chapter 5 "U.S. Foreign Policy in the South China Sea," examines why the SCS has become the most dangerous spot on the globe. Some $5 trillion worth of trade moves through it annually, yet several states, including the People's Republic of China (PRC), Malaysia, the Philippines, Vietnam, Indonesia, and the Republic of China (Taiwan) (ROC) make territorial claims, and many non-claimant states, including the United States, want the waters to remain international and routinely conduct "freedom of navigation" operations to punctuate that position. The chapter examines the viability of the territorial claims and explores the consequences of any change in the status quo and uses a variety of case studies that are going to be relevant to the area. The chapter answers the following question: if the PRC were to gain control over key areas, how would it affect its neighbors, and what would the future of free trade in the region look like? Last but not least, the author explains Beijing's relationship with the United States and warns if either the U.S. or the PRC were to push its point of view, consequences for global peace would be dire.

The Chapter 6, "One Belt One Road: A Bargain in the South China Sea Disputes," critically examines the One Belt One Road (OBOR) strategy (with special reference to the China–Pakistan Economic Corridor), and analyzes whether it can act as a bargain, and even a "soft" balancing strategy in the SCS and be a "game-changer" both in the regional sphere and on the global stage. The chapter discusses whether the Belt and Road Initiative (BRI) can significantly alter Asia's emerging international order, and even accelerate contests and forge cooperation in the region. This chapter also briefly examines the China–Pakistan Economic Corridor as a case study, and explores whether Beijing's assertive policies in the South China Sea and OBOR are contradictory. Finally, the chapter concludes with a brief summary of the results of the bargain and its possible implications in Asian geopolitics.

The concluding chapter summarizes the findings of the study, considers various policies that might at least help to lessen tensions in the SCS region, and suggests several avenues of future research that might prove fruitful for policymakers and/or academics. The volume demonstrates trenchant analysis while focusing on the region's foreign policy, alliance patterns, domestic Chinese politics, as well as discussing the policy responses of key Indo-Pacific actors. Finally, the book concludes with the hope expressed by Sun Tzu that "*winning one hundred victories in one hundred battles is not the acme of skill. Rather, subduing the enemy without fighting is the acme of skill.*" [1]

References

1. Tzu, S. (2007). *The Art of War.* Filiquarian; First Thus edition.
2. Damon, E. (2020). Beijing harasses Petronas and Shell off Malaysia. https://www.energyvoice.com/oilandgas/asia/237214/beijing-harasses-petronas-and-shell-off-malaysiamal/.

https://doi.org/10.1142/9781786349286_0002

Chapter 2

China's Geoeconomic Diplomacy and the South China Sea Dispute: Promises and Pitfalls

Romi Jain

2.1 Introduction

China's "reemergence" as an influential economic power from the ashes of history has shifted "the world economy's center of gravity to East Asia." [11] Key facts illustrate this. Over the 2005–2018 period, China's worldwide investments and construction activities amounted to US$1.87 trillion, marking an uptick from US$548.69 billion and US$1321.9 billion in 2005–2011 and 2012–2018, respectively [47]. China no longer enjoys a double-digit economic growth rate, which it did in the 2000s, and has rather embraced the "new normal" approach of sustainable growth. However, it is the world's second largest economy, and its gross domestic product (GDP), valued at US$14.17 trillion in 2019, accounts for 16% of the global economy [2]. Moreover, China ranks first in economic relationships and second in economic resources (economic size, international leverage, technology, and connectivity) in the Asia Power Index, which measures national power of countries, including the United States, in the Asia-Pacific region [33]. Economic relationships measure the "ability to wield influence through economic outreach and interdependencies" such as China's trade and investment relations with and development assistance to the Asia-Pacific region. Notably, East Asia, including Southeast Asia, is considered China-led, following the "first wave" of the

Japan-centric region, inasmuch as the Chinese economy fuels East Asia's growth engine and because China has emerged as a regional "integrator" through its global and regional production networks [6].

With its growing economic clout, China is vigorously practicing economic statecraft in achieving its foreign policy goals. No exception to its application is the South China Sea, a resource-rich region of 3.5 million-square-kilometer waterway, extending from the Strait of Malacca to the Strait of Taiwan [46]. It is known as the 9-dash area that is claimed by China, while competing claims have been put forth by Vietnam, Malaysia, the Philippines, Brunei, Indonesia, Singapore, and Taiwan.

It may be clarified that China has not abjured military means. This is evident from its regular deployment of maritime "military militia," [21] militarization of the Spratly Islands, as well as such belligerent episodes as the Johnson South Reef skirmish with Vietnam in the Spratly Islands in 1988, the 1995 occupation of the Mischief Reef within the Philippines's Exclusive Economic Zone (EEZ), and the 2012 Scarborough Shoal standoff with the Philippines. Moreover, Beijing has built artificial islands in the Paracel and Spratly Island chains, carrying radar facilities and airstrips [16]. Hence, the rationale of economic instruments in China's foreign policy toolkit is to complement military measures. It advances national interests through a slew of tools, inclusive of trade and investment-driven networks, and turning rivals into partners and dependents, thereby blunting their opposition and eliciting cooperation on contentious issues.

In keeping with the above background, this chapter critically examines China's geoeconomic strategy *vis-à-vis* Vietnam and the Philippines, the major contenders, in mellowing their assertions over the South China Sea issue and in guarding Beijing's exclusive claim. The other Southeast Asian claimants figure in occasional references in the chapter. The chapter is organized as follows. While the first part discusses the geoeconomics theory, the second part assesses the strength of China's geoeconomic diplomacy and illustrates the success areas and promising moves. The third part identifies the weak spots and challenges to geoeconomics. The final part concludes.

2.2 The Geoeconomics Theory

Owing perhaps to sheer ascendancy of economics in the post-Cold War international politics, scholars and policymakers have latched on to geoeconomics as a convenient nomenclature. But they hold varied notions of this elastic phrase and have failed to differentiate between "geo-economics and geopolitics" and explain "the 'geo' in geo-economics." [5] In their threadbare analysis, therefore, Scholvin and Wigell [2018] condense geoeconomics to both statecraft and an analytical approach [5]. The first entails the use of economic tools in achieving "geo-strategic objectives" or "geopolitical results," [9] whereas as an analytical prism, geoeconomics has both realist and liberal underpinnings.

From the realist perspective, Luttwak [1990] reasons that states have "to act 'geo-economically' simply because of what they are: spatially-defined entities structured to outdo each other on the world scene that uses the logic of war in the grammar of commerce." [3] Similarly, Gilpin opines that "realism today necessarily means neo-mercantilism." [10] In the same vein, in the context of rising mercantilism worldwide, resulting in the subordination of fair international trade to national economic policies, Malmgren wrote in Foreign Policy as early as 1970, "Economics [is going to be] powerful politics. Neo-mercantilism will be its scourge, driving nations into international conflicts, as have ideologies and military imbalances in the past." [12]

In other words, this viewpoint situates power struggle predominantly in the economic domain, with trade wars being its characteristic manifestation. The ongoing U.S.–China trade war serves as its prime example, though geoeconomics will fit in this picture if the tussle is located in a geographically significant context.

From the liberalist perspective, geoeconomics involves win–win propositions in the age of interdependence, reflecting inter-state cooperation in the spirit of shared gains. For instance, under the banner of the Belt and Road Initiative (BRI) China has couched its scientific collaborations in this framework: whether it be the 16+1 group (Cooperation between China and Central and East European Countries), or the China–Pakistan Economic Corridor, stated to be both uplifting for China's western regions and critical for Pakistan's economic development.

Given that China as an emerging world power employs a motley of approaches in its foreign policy, its geoeconomic policy is not restricted to an exclusive frame of realism or liberalism. Its practices reflect two distinct though mutually reinforcing layers of geoeconomics. First, *geoeconomics in service to geopolitics*: as statecraft, it is the exercise of economic diplomacy toward rival claimants of the South China Sea in vindicating its exclusive claim to the South China Sea. Second, *military means in service to geoeconomics*: given the salience of the South China Sea for its oil and natural gas wealth, China has simultaneously utilized muscular means [17] to ward off the other claimants. For example, on account of China's military threats, Vietnam suspended oil projects awarded to Repsol, a foreign firm, for operations in the South China Sea [40]. The second layer is the realist geoeconomics undergirded by zero-sum economic gains. The first layer is actually the geoeconomic strategy or statecraft, which constitutes the focus of this chapter.

2.3 Strengths of China's Geoeconomic Strategy

China's prestige as an economic power has had a multiplier effect, including among claimants to the South China Sea. With the launch of the mega project, the Belt and Road Initiative (BRI), economic relationship with China has become even more alluring even though the controversy over the host countries ending up in a "debt trap" has surfaced. Harnessing its economic position, China has attempted to "foster asymmetrical economic dependence on China … and once that is achieved to shape their foreign policies in ways congenial to China's national interests." [7, 9] The prospect of prosperity is what China has stimulated through trade and investments. On the flip side, economic coercion is at work to curb the practices inimical to China's national interest.

Torrecampo [2019] articulates the long-term implications for the South China Sea dispute:

> allowing China, through its associates, to participate in investments on critical industries and infrastructure hands them a clear leverage in any dispute or conflict that may arise between China and the Philippines. The economic clout built carefully by Beijing can be used as a tool to push the Philippines into submission even before conflict erupts or to prevent the latter from countering the former. [50]

Similarly, Tran [2015] concludes that Vietnam's economic dependency on China will make it factor in economic considerations more than the "sovereignty concern" in its response to China's threat [4, 51]. Be that as it may, it is worth examining what China has accomplished so far, and what threats and challenges lie ahead on its geoeconomic path.

2.3.1 *Economic incentives and the Philippines' "appeasement" policy*

In July 2016, the Philippines and the United States scored a momentous victory in international arbitration that ruled out the legal basis of China's historical rights over the 9-dash line resources. Yet Philippine President Rodrigo Roa Duterte was reluctant to antagonize China by enforcing the ruling and distanced away from the United States instead. Later, in April 2018, under Beijing's pressure, phrased as "friendly" advice, he revoked his decision to unfurl the Philippine flag in the Sea. Interestingly, his regime is equally applying the geoeconomic approach toward China in order to stave off skirmishes and armed conflict in the South China Sea. Hinting at the significance of trade and commercial ties with China, therefore, Hermogenes Esperon, Duterte's main security adviser, stated: "[O]ur relations (with China) are not only about the South China Sea or the West Philippine Sea. There are many other aspects." [32]

Commenting on the power of purse, Renato Cruz De Castro, a professor in the international studies department of De La Salle University, Manila, attributes President Duterte's "appeasement policy" toward China to the allure of the BRI. He observes, "Duterte and his economic advisers saw how Chinese investments boosted infrastructure development in Myanmar, Laos and Cambodia … Duterte was afraid that the Philippines would not be able to avail of the BRI's economic benefits if it challenges China's expansionist agenda in the South China Sea." [32] Furthermore, at the Boao Forum for Asia Annual Convention, held in Hainan on March 26–29, 2019, House Speaker Gloria Macapagal-Arroyo glorified the Chinese development model:

> China has given us the lesson that there is just not one path for development. Prior to China's experience, it was thought that the only way to development is the Western-Style model of Jeffersonian democracy coupled with a free market … But China has shown the world that you can have your own model of development using your own historical experience. [49]

Moreover, Philippine Foreign Affairs Secretary Teodoro Locsin stated that the prospect of a strategic partnership with China was "more attractive than the current offer of the U.S. of strategic confusion" and stressed that Manila's defense treaty with the United States did not "preclude" economic ties with China. In fact, Locsin expressed concern that the Philippines had woefully lagged behind other countries in integrating with the Chinese economy [13]. But he added a caveat that Manila would not give up its claim to the South China Sea since "surrender is never an option." [13]

In the latest developments in June 2019, tensions ratcheted up over China's sinking of a Philippine fishing boat in the South China Sea. China refuted the Philippine claim that it was intentional. It is speculated that if it were purposive, it could be the result of China's reaction to the recent spurt in Manila's bonhomie with Tokyo and the United States or it could be Beijing's strategy to assess the level of Philippines' reaction and countermeasures. In any case, the initial infuriation-coated statements of President Duterte ebbed within a month when he "played down" the ramming, saying it was "a maritime incident … there was no confrontation … there was no bloody violence." [24]

2.3.1.1 *"Build, build, build" and other deals*

In fact, a chronicle of events demonstrates the Philippines' inclination toward China. At the invitation of President Duterte, Chinese President Xi Jinping paid a state visit to the Philippines in November 2018. According to the Joint Statement released on November 21, 2018, "both sides reaffirmed that contentious issues are not the sum total of China-Philippines bilateral relations" as well as affirming "the importance of the Bilateral Consultation Mechanism on the South China Sea and the Maritime Cooperation Joint Committee between the two Coast Guards." [31] The statement was supplemented by as many as 29 MoUs and agreements for bilateral cooperation on the BRI and in fields of oil and gas development, economic and technical cooperation, infrastructure, industrial parks, China Aid Bridge and Road Project, and other areas [31]. During his visit, President Xi also assured President Duterte with financing the infrastructural program "Build, Build, Build Initiative" which is considered a decisive factor in nudging Duterte to toe the China line, for instance, acquiescing in not raising the Philippines flag in the South China Sea. Accordingly, China is a key funder to the Philippines' project of transforming the Clark base, a former American military base, into a city [35]. Timothy McLaughlin comments in *The Atlantic* in this context, "This redevelopment of a former symbol of American might here in Clark by a Chinese developer may be the best example of the shift under way in

Southeast Asia, as a more assertive Beijing courts traditional American allies in a part of the world where Washington's power long went unchallenged."

In April 2019, President Duterte visited Beijing to attend the second Belt and Road Forum. His business delegation signed as many as 19 business deals with Chinese firms amounting to P633 billion ($12.16 billion) mainly in "energy, infrastructure, food, telecommunications, tourism, and economic zone development," expecting to "generate over 21,000 jobs" [36]. Examples include an $800-million contract agreement for the proposed 250MW South Pulangi Hydroelectric Power Plant Project; a framework agreement for thermal, hydro, and renewable power plants worth at least $1.5 billion; and memoranda of understanding related to a petrochemical refinery processing plant complex, construction of the Light Rail Transit, construction of infrastructure for nationwide Wi-Fi Internet connectivity, and the development of the economic zone; and a purchase framework agreement for the supply of $40 million worth of pineapples to Beijing [36]. It is speculated that the BBB program could be another case of the alleged "debt trap" policy of China. This diplomacy involves enticing poorer countries with reasonable loans for infrastructure development and extracting concessions or gains "in exchange for debt relief." [34] The case of Sri Lanka's handover of the Hambantota Port to China because of its inability to repay the debt is a frequently cited instance.

2.3.1.2 *Coercive economic measures*

Indeed, the turnaround in the Philippines' relations with China is characteristic of the Duterte presidency. Beijing's use of coercive economic tools was prominent in Manila's preceding regime.[a] Let us consider, for example, the developments following the Philippines–China standoff over the Scarborough Shoal, a "cluster of islands" around 220 km off the coast of

[a]Some scholars include cyber-attacks in geoeconomic instruments. But the author agrees with Col. Troxell's observation, "Cyberattacks clearly represent a significant security threat, and in many cases, these attacks target critical components of economic infrastructure and industry, but the examination of this aspect of statecraft should have its own platform and not necessarily be considered a geoeconomic event." See Col. John F. Troxell, "Geoeconomics," Military Review, January-February 2018, https://www.armyupress.army.mil/Journals/Military-Review/English-Edition-Archives/January-February-2018/Geoeconomics/.

the Philippines. China blacklisted as many as 27 Filipino fruit exporters, imposing in May 2012 a ban on banana exports from the Philippines for whom China was a critical market. Nearly 200,000 people faced the prospect of losing jobs as a result. Moreover, Pilipino Banana Growers and Exporters Association (PBGEA) member companies reported that "six to seven million boxes per year or 20–25% of their total production was lost due to suspension order … before the suspension order sometime in 2010–2012, exports to China grew by 20–30% per annum."[b] Though officially, discovery of pests in imports was cited as a justification for the quarantine, its timing suggested retribution [8]. Scholars like Ba and Storey [2016] dispute its connection with the South China Sea issue by pointing out that phytosanitary measures were indeed the concern of the Chinese government. However, given that "coercive economic diplomacy" is not new to Chinese foreign policy practices [25], linkages with the South China Sea issue cannot be completely ruled out.

In addition, it may be recalled that the Chinese government had issued in 2012 an "advisory" to its citizens against traveling to the Philippines, which was lifted during President Duterte's visit to China in October 2016 that was aimed to mend the ruptured ties over the Sea dispute. Notably, the Philippine government has been aggressively harnessing the country's sterling strength in tourism to drive economic growth. According to the Philippine Statistics Authority (PSA), in 2017, the tourism sector contributed 12.2% to the country's GDP and directly accounted for 13.1% of the country's employment [45]. Furthermore, the government's long-term vision for development and prosperity, known as AmBisyon Natin 2040, envisages a significant role of tourism and allied services. Notably, China ranks second to South Korea as a source of the Philippines-bound tourists: according to the Philippine Department of Tourism, "a total of 463,804 Chinese tourists visited the Philippines from January to March [2019], or 24.87% more than the 371,429 recorded in the first three months of 2018." [52] It is speculated that China's 40% stake in the National Grid Corporation of the Philippines (NGCP) empowers it to shut off the grid, should a high-handed tactic be required [23]. Basically, tourism and fruit exports have had been subjected to China's restrictions as part of its coercive [4] geoeconomic strategy toward the Philippines, though the

[b]China revoked the ban in October 2016. Ace June Rells S. Perez, "China Lifts Banana Ban," Sun Star, October 18, 2016, https://www.sunstar.com.ph/article/104874.

Duterte regime has been offered more of inducements and incentives for being accommodative.

2.3.2 *Trade dependence*

A predominant share of Vietnam's exports is sustained by the Chinese market, while many Vietnamese industries, including textile and footwear exporters, rely on imports of Chinese raw materials and equipment for manufacturing [1]. According to the General Statistics Office of Vietnam, Vietnam's preliminary exports to and imports from China in 2017 amounted to US$35.46 billion and US$52.54 billion, respectively, rising to US$41.27 billion and US$65.44 billion in 2018, respectively. The volume of exports and imports in 2019, January through April, was US$10.47 billion and US$22.77 billion, respectively. Given the Sino-Vietnam trade picture, Blackwill and Harris (2016) make the following observation, "China's economic hold over Vietnam is such that Hanoi remains more vulnerable than Manila to Chinese coercion: Vietnam is highly dependent upon the PRC [People's Republic of China] for rubber, and major Chinese imports are used in the goods Vietnam ultimately exports. Unlike the Philippines, Vietnam does not enjoy a mutual defense treaty with the United States. Perhaps not coincidentally, China's claims in the South China Sea are particularly aggressive toward Vietnam, threatening 70% of Vietnam's exclusive economic zone — not particularly auspicious for a country so reliant on fishing as a food source." [9]

Indeed, Vietnam protested China's annual fishing ban, in force from May through August 2019, in the South China Sea on the ground that it violates Hanoi's sovereignty over the Paracel Islands [41]. In fact, this unilateral practice of Beijing has been in place since 1999, whose purported aim is to protect the ocean ecosystem and biodiversity, but which also reinforces Beijing's exclusive jurisdiction over the Sea.

2.3.3 *Picking the low-hanging fruits*

Among the claimants to the South China Sea, Brunei, with a claim only to a 200-nautical mile Exclusive Economic Zone (EEZ), has been passive and quiet. It is conjectured that its "silence" is the price for the expected lucrative returns. Following a gap of 13 years, Chinese President Xi Jinping was the first Chinese head of state to pay a state visit to Brunei in

November 2018. Aiming to consolidate cordial ties, Xi welcomed expansion of its exports to China and affirmed the latter's willingness to strengthen bilateral cooperation in areas of infrastructure, agriculture, fishery, and energy [52]. President Xi reiterated China's appreciation for Brunei's "dual-track approach" to the South China Sea dispute. Further, a bilateral protocol agreement was signed between the two countries in June 2019 for the export of wild aquatic food to China. Notably, 34% of Brunei's aquatic products were exported to China in 2018. Importantly, it may be noted that China is a "dominant partner" in implementing Brunei's economic restructuring plan, *Brunei Vision 2035* (*or Wawasan 2035*), funding infrastructure projects such as the oil refinery and petrochemical complex currently [26]. With their ties lifted to the "strategic cooperative partnership" plane, both sides are aligning the synergies of the BRI project and Vision 2035.

It is an open truth that Malaysia previously embraced a "bandwagoning" [14] approach on the dispute, attributable to China's sterling influence in both military and economic terms. But compared to Brunei, Malaysia is less pliable on the issue, especially under the leadership of Prime Minister Mahathis Mohamad. For instance, Kuala Lumpur has reiterated its demand for non-militarization of the Sea, for the freedom of navigation [29], and for an ASEAN-centric solution rather than a bilateral one. Nevertheless, Malaysia recognizes the significance of economic tie-up with China, which is not only its largest trading partner but is also an enticing investor. The Malaysia–China Kuantan Industrial Park (MCKIP) is gaining in momentum and is likely to attract nearly 20 billion ringgits (US$4.8 billion) in investments [48]. Further, Malaysian Economic Affairs Minister Azmin Ali stated at the China Conference in Kuala Lumpur, October 2018, "Today we expect China to provide global leadership not just in the economic sphere but in soft power by advancing universal values such as freedom of conscience, mutual respect, and justice."

2.3.4 *Energy diplomacy*

China clinched a major strategic gain when during his visits to Brunei and the Philippines in November 2018, President Xi signed with each country the memorandum of understanding (MoU) for joint oil and gas exploration and development in the South China Sea [43]. Beijing and Manila are at work on finalizing the related framework.

The Philippines's massive need for the South China Sea's oil and gas resources is considered to be driving the joint exploration decision, given that its key gas deposit at Malampaya, off Palawan Island, is expected to deplete by 2030. Also, its prospects for exploring Reed Bank in the South China Sea have been thwarted under China's duress [43]. Defending the MoU, Philippine Ambassador to China Jose Santiago Sta. Roman stated:

> our bilateral relations basically consist of two general areas — the disputes and the areas where there are no disputes. The disputes do not define everything. They're only a part of the overall picture. So, where there are no disputes, like trade, economics, science, culture, we're able to fast-track. Where there are disputes, we discuss through diplomatic channels or through the bilateral consultative mechanism. [18] Notwithstanding Manila's imperative need for energy security, opposition parties in the Philippines have reprobated the MoU on the grounds that it is tantamount to recognizing the "unlawful 'co-ownership' with China of the West Philippine Sea [or the South China Sea]."

However, the ruling Philippine government considers it both pragmatic and necessary to partner with China for both energy security and for not being totally pushed out of the South China Sea zone by antagonizing the militarily powerful Beijing. Nevertheless, it is the final agreement that will be likely to clarify what specific "outcomes" of exploration are intended for both parties, which is not clear from the current MoU. For its part, Beijing uses energy cooperation as an instrument of reward to less vocal claimants to the South China Sea as well as a means to "demonstrate the efficacy of bilateral arrangements." [42]

2.3.5 *Regulations on the development of uninhabited islands*

Hainan Province's Department of Ocean and Fisheries issued a regulation in July 2018 on the development of uninhabited islands, requiring interested entities or individuals to submit applications and plans to ocean administration authorities. According to *ChinaDaily*, July 5, 2018, the regulation specified durations are 15 years for cultivation, 25 years for tourism and entertainment, 30 years for salt and mining industries, and 40 years for public welfare purposes [15]. By wielding the power to sanction development, it is a strategic move to legitimize China's jurisdiction [53]. In fact, Chen Xiangmiao, a research fellow at the state-supported

National Institute for the South China Sea, unambiguously stated, "The development on uninhabited islands will maintain stability of (the) South China Sea and dispel other countries' attempts to invade and occupy our territorial sovereignty." [30]

2.4 Challenges and Weak Spots

Several constraints such as economic diversification, the U.S. role, the BRI image, and the domestic factors affect the efficacy of China's geoeconomic diplomacy.

2.4.1 *Trade and investment diversification*

The Philippines's economic dependency on China is not as high as that of Vietnam and Malaysia. China is neither its "top direct investor" nor a top export market [37]. As for the BBB program, if China were to be the sole participant or financier, Manila would have been running the risk of being caught in the debt and dependency web. But in view of Japan's involvement in the project and its increased trade and investment cooperation with Manila, the latter is clearly abstaining from putting all its eggs in one basket. Similarly, efforts are underway in Vietnam in getting away from dependency. In fact, in the aftermath of the U.S.–China trade war, Vietnam's economy has received a boost as foreign manufacturing operations are shifting from China to Vietnam. Other than that, Vietnam's low labor wages make it an appealing manufacturing base. In addition, Vietnam is proactively diversifying trade and economic cooperation, signing the free trade agreement with the European Union (EU) in June 2019, apart from clinching high-tech defense deals with Washington. For example, it has ratified the Comprehensive and Progressive Agreement for Trans-Pacific Partnership (CPTPP), primarily in order to diminish reliance on China [20]. Bennett Murray makes the following apt observation in *Foreign Policy*:

> … with China likely to remain a rival to the West for the foreseeable future, Vietnam's willingness to get along with power centers in North America and Europe provides a political advantage that's unlikely to vanish, and its growing strategic partnership with the Pentagon links the U.S. bilateral economic relationship with defense. Already climbing the

ladder of the global supply chain and willing to make reforms to accommodate free trade agreements, Vietnam has become not just a cheaper but also a friendlier alternative to China in the Trump era. [38]

Moreover, in view of perceived security threat from China as well as to prevent dependence on Chinese technology, Vietnam's Viettel has opted for 5G without involving Huawei and develop its own "5G chips and core network infrastructure." [27] However, the Philippines's Global Telecoms launched the 5G broadband service with equipment such as modems provided by Huawei. Hence, there is no coordinated counter-response to China's attempts at intensifying its economic penetration into Southeast Asian economies for strategic purposes.

2.4.2 *Maligned image of the BRI*

Even though the Philippines has welcomed Chinese investment in its infrastructure projects, the image of the BRI as a debt entanglement could make Manila or any other claimant countries turn cynical in committing to a future project with China, should more debt trap stories come to the fore. Ironically, in order to impart strength to economic diplomacy, China needs to prove its professed belief in win–win outcomes, while at the same time, extracting geopolitical concessions through manipulative economic practices could be the aim of its investment diplomacy. Thus, Beijing would find it challenging to walk this tightrope.

2.4.3 *The U.S. factor*

The first quarter of 2019 witnessed a modicum of enhanced assertiveness in President Duterte's postures, mainly on account of the Trump administration's defense assurance as well as its diplomatic pressure. As China scaled up dispatch of vessels near "Philippines-occupied Thitu Island" (or Pag-asa Island), President Duterte firmly stated that both parties needed to demonstrate "mutual respect for sovereignty." Encouraged by Secretary of State Mike Pence's clarification that in the event of attack on the Philippines, the United States would resort to the Mutual Defense Treaty, the Philippines conducted drills along with the United States, India, and Japan in the South China Sea in May 2019. Also, in view of the domestic elections, strong statements on the sovereignty issue poured in from President Duterte [39], such as "I will not plead or beg, but I am just telling you that lay off the Pag-asa because I have soldiers there. If you touch it, that's another story. Then I will tell my soldiers 'prepare for suicide missions.'" [28]

2.4.4 *Domestic forces*

The domestic constituencies in Vietnam and the Philippines countervail the drift into China's orb. In June 2019, the Philippines high court directed the Philippine Navy, police, and the Coast Guard to protect reefs and marine life in Scarborough Shoal, Second Thomas Shoal, and Mischief Reef [44]. Similarly, Antonio Carpio, a Supreme Court justice and a South China Sea expert, has prodded the Philippines government to take the fishing boat incident seriously, stating that it was "a quantum escalation of China's aggressive acts." [24] Further, owing to the lack of trust in China's intentions, the Philippine Senate disapproved the proposal for Chinese supplies for the Department of the Interior and Local Government's surveillance systems [19].

Similarly, nationalistic sentiments are seething in Vietnam. As Ravindram observes, "The ruling elite in Vietnam would have to consider the domestic cost of compliance with sanctions initiated by China. In other words, the incentive for the political class to comply with targeted sanctions against them would most likely be offset by nationalistic sentiments in Vietnam." [4] This is corroborated by the Vietnamese government's botched attempt to enact the law to create three special economic zones (SEZs) in Van Don, North Van Phong, and Phu Quoc. Government advisor Võ Trí Thành stated that the proposed law's purpose was "to create a leading edge for the country's growth in the face of a scarcity of resources, and political and social complexities." [22]

However, the Vietnamese public opposed the move, apprehending neo-colonialism taking shape with Chinese economic intervention. Also, many Vietnamese economists argue that Chinese investors' primary interest is in "casinos and resorts" [21], as the example of Cambodia suggests, whereas Vietnam needs hi-tech investment. As a result, the proposal is hanging in the air. It may be added that in terms of investment, China accounts for only 5.8% of total foreign direct investment in Vietnam, ranking behind South Korea, Japan, and Singapore. With SEZs, China's position in Vietnam could become more strategic. Regardless of the domestic pressures, however, the Philippine government led by President Duterte has applied a more placating approach, barring sporadic assertive postures.

2.5 Conclusion

Based on the foregoing examination, key upshots are outlined. First, from time to time, China has utilized seductive, ingenious, and coercive economic mechanisms to vindicate its claim to the 9-dash area in the South China Sea. It is not to suggest that the geoeconomic diplomacy is potent enough to drive Vietnam and the Philippines to part with their claims to the South China Sea, since doing so would require an imperative *raison d'être* for the latter. However, economic considerations have certainly impacted the tone and tenor of their reactions to issues and incidents involving the South China Sea. For example, despite the acrimonious moment in the China–Philippines relations over the boat sinking issue, Manila was discreet enough not to let it impair the blossoming economic ties. In justification, Presidential Spokesman Salvador Panelo stated that President Duterte was "making his enemies friends so that both sides will mutually gain benefit from whatever they have." [36] In fact, Duterte threatened to imprison his critics, castigating him for his soft approach, should they attempted to impeach him.

Second, a determining factor for the geoeconomic strategy to succeed would be the level of economic dependence of the claimant countries on China. From this perspective, China encounters several challenges such as Vietnam's efforts to neutralize China's economic leverage through trade diversification as well as anti-China sentiments flaring up in pockets of Manila and Hanoi. Nevertheless, Vietnam and the Philippines are faced with hard choices, facing a trade-off between the enticing Chinese investments and their strategic necessity to shake off any deepening dependency. Moreover, Vietnam will need to address its "labor and skills shortage" as it prepares to become a prominent global manufacturing platform.

Third, geoeconomics is essentially tied to a "larger geopolitical agenda." It might not deliver immediate results but, over time, as the economies of the claimant states intertwine with China's (or as the "asymmetrical dependence" sharpens), China could be in a position to reap strategic benefits. Importantly, Beijing has made long-term canny moves to fortify its exclusive claims to the South China Sea: its offer of joint oil and gas exploration to pliant claimants, annual fishing moratoriums, and regulations for development of uninhabited islands signify spiraling of allocative authority at the vortex of Beijing's leadership.

References

1. Binh, N. X. (2017). Main characteristics of Vietnam–China trade relations, 2000–15. *China Report, 53*(3), 355–366. doi: 10.1177/0009445517711510.
2. Jain, R. (2018). China's economic expansion in South Asia: Strengths, challenges and opportunities. *Indian Journal of Asian Affairs, 31*(1–2), 21–36.
3. Luttwak, E. N. (1990). From geopolitics to geo-economics: Logic of conflict, grammar of commerce. *The National Interest*, (20), 17–23.
4. Ravindran, M. S. (2012). Chinas potential for economic coercion in the South China Sea disputes: A comparative study of the Philippines and Vietnam. *Journal of Current Southeast Asian Affairs, 31*(3), 105–132. doi: 10.1177/186810341203100305.
5. Scholvin, S. & Wigell, M. (2018). Power politics by economic means: Geoeconomics as an analytical approach and foreign policy practice. *Comparative Strategy, 37*(1), 73–84. doi: 10.1080/01495933.2018.1419729.
6. Wong, J. (2013). A China-centric economic order in East Asia. *Asia Pacific Business Review, 19*(2), 286–296. doi: 10.1080/13602381.2012.739358.
7. Wu, F. & Wei, K. D. (2014). From financial assets to financial statecraft: The case of China and emerging economies of Africa and Latin America. *Journal ofContemporaryChina,23*(89),781–803.doi:10.1080/10670564.2014.882533.
8. Ba, A. & Storey, I. (2016). Continuity and change in the South China Sea. In C. Jenner & T. Thuy (Eds.), *The South China Sea: A Crucible of Regional Cooperation or Conflict-making Sovereignty Claims?* (pp. 71–96). Cambridge: Cambridge University Press. doi:10.1017/CBO9781139963084.006.
9. Blackwill, R. D. & Harris, J. M. (2016). *War by Other Means: Geoeconomics and Statecraft*. Cambridge, MA: Harvard University Press.
10. Diesen, G. (2017). *Russia's geoeconomic strategy for a greater Eurasia.* (p. 13). Routledge Ltd.
11. Jenkins, R. (2019). *How China is Reshaping the Global Economy: Development Impacts in Africa and Latin America.* (p. 1). Oxford University Press.
12. Malmgren, H. B. (1970). Coming Trade Wars? (Neo-Mercantilism and Foreign Policy). *Foreign Policy*, 1, 143. doi: 10.2307/1147892.
13. Calonzo, A. & Jiao, C. (2019). Philippines prefers China loans over U.S. "strategic confusion" in South China Sea. *Bloomberg*. https://www.

bloomberg.com/news/articles/2019-05-20/china-has-more-to-offer-than-u-s-top-philippine-diplomat-says.

14. Carpenter, T. G. (2016). What are the Philippines and Malaysia doing when it comes to China? (It's called bandwagoning). *National Interest.* https://nationalinterest.org/feature/what-are-the-philippines-malaysia-doing-when-it-comes-china-18298.
15. Chi, M. (2018). Hainan allows private firms to develop islands. *China Daily.* http://www.chinadaily.com.cn/a/201807/05/WS5b3d7e1ea3103349141e0d4a.html.
16. CNN. (2018). Duterte will "go to war" over South China Sea resources, minister says. https://m.cnn.com/en/article/h_c5fc0d8130d71e6f521e9d2b583ea2fd.
17. Cronin, P. M. & Stires, H. (2018). China is Waging a Maritime Insurgency in the South China Sea. It's Time for the United States to Counter It. *National Interest.* https://nationalinterest.org/feature/china-waging-maritime-insurgency-south-china-sea-its-time-united-states-counter-it-28062.
18. Dumlao-Abadilla, D. (2019). PH, China oil pact still a go. *Inquirer* https://business.inquirer.net/269161/ph-china-oil-pact-still-a-go.
19. Elemia, C. (2018). Senators sound alarm over China-funded DILG surveillance project. *Rappler.* https://www.rappler.com/nation/218831-dilg-china-telecom-affiliate-partnership-video-surveillance-system-philippines.
20. Elmer, K. (2018). Vietnam becomes seventh nation to adopt new Trans-Pacific Partnership. *South China Morning Post.* https://www.scmp.com/news/china/diplomacy/article/2172939/vietnam-steers-between-us-and-china-ratifying-trade-deal.
21. Esmaquel, P. (2019). China deploys militia as Philippines builds on Pag-asa Island. *Rappler,* Retrieved from https://www.rappler.com/nation/222916-china-deploys-militia-philippines-builds-on-pagasa-island.
22. Fawthrop, T. (2019). Public criticism pressures Vietnam to back down on new economic zones. *China Dialogue.* https://chinadialogue.net/en/business/11154-public-criticism-pressures-vietnam-to-back-down-on-new-economic-zones/.
23. Griffiths, J. (2019). China can shut off the Philippines' power grid at any time, leaked report warns. *CNN.* https://edition.cnn.com/2019/11/25/asia/philippines-china-power-grid-intl-hnk/index.html.
24. Gutierrez, J. (2019). Duterte Plays Down Chinese Ramming of Philippine Fishing Boat. *New York Times.* https://www.nytimes.com/2019/06/25/world/asia/philippines-china-duterte-ships.html.
25. Harrell, P., Rosenberg, E., & Saravalle, E. (2018). China's Use of Coercive Economic Measures. *Center for a New American Security.* https://www.cnas.org/publications/reports/chinas-use-of-coercive-economic-measures.

26. Hart, M. (2018). Brunei Abandons South China Sea Claim for Chinese Finance. *Geopolitical Monitor*. https://www.geopoliticalmonitor.com/brunei-abandons-south-china-sea-claim-for-chinese-finance/.
27. Hiep, L. H. (2019). Vietnam races to launch 5g network, but Chinese tech giant Huawei notably left out of plan. *South China Morning Post.* https://www.scmp.com/week-asia/opinion/article/3008714/vietnam-races-launch-5g-network-chinese-tech-giant-huawei-notably.
28. HKFP. (2020). "I will tell my soldiers to prepare for suicide missions": Philippines' Duterte warns China to back off disputed island. *HKFP.* https://www.hongkongfp.com/2019/04/05/i-will-tell-soldiers-prepare-suicide-missions-philippines-duterte-warns-china-back-off-disputed-island/.
29. Jaipragas, B. (2018). Malaysia looks to Chinese leadership, but not on South China Sea. *South China Morning Post.* https://www.scmp.com/week-asia/geopolitics/article/2168119/malaysia-looks-chinese-leadership-not-south-china-sea.
30. Johnson, J. (2018). China's Hainan province invites "individuals" to develop uninhabited islands in South China Sea. *Japan Times.* https://www.japantimes.co.jp/news/2018/07/07/asia-pacific/chinas-hainan-province-invites-individuals-develop-uninhabited-islands-south-china-sea/.
31. Joint Philippines-China Statement on the State Visit of Chinese President Xi Jinping to the Philippines, Department of Foreign Affairs, Republic of the Philippines, November 21, 2018. https://dfa.gov.ph/dfa-news/statements-and-advisoriesupdate/18537-philippines-china-joint-statement-on-the-state-visit-of-chinese-president-xi-jinping-to-the-philippines.
32. Kyodo. (2019). The Philippines' Rodrigo Duterte broached South China Sea ruling in meeting with China's Xi Jinping. *The Japan Times*. https://www.japantimes.co.jp/news/2019/04/28/asia-pacific/politics-diplomacy-asia-pacific/philippines-rodrigo-duterte-broached-south-china-sea-ruling-meeting-chinas-xi-jinping/#.XNyRg45KjIU.
33. Lowy Institute. (2019). Asia Power Index: China. Retrieved from https://power.lowyinstitute.org/countries.php?profile=46.
34. Mantesso, S. (2018). What happens when poorer nations lured by China's cheap loans can't pay them back? *ABC News*. https://www.abc.net.au/news/2018-11-16/are-china-cheap-loans-to-poor-nations-a-debt-trap/10493286.
35. McLaughlin, T. (2019). A U.S. Ally Is Turning to China to "Build, Build, Build." *The Atlantic*. https://www.theatlantic.com/international/archive/2019/05/philippines-us-ally-china-investment/588829/.
36. Merez, A. (2019). PH inks P633 billion in trade, investment deals with China. *ABS-CBN News*. https://news.abs-cbn.com/business/04/26/19/ph-inks-p633-billion-in-trade-investment-deals-with-china.
37. Mourdoukoutas, P. (2019). Philippines Can Escape From China — There's Still Time. *Forbes*. https://www.forbes.com/sites/panosmourdoukoutas/

2019/05/04/philippines-can-escape-from-china-theres-still-time/#3bad04e337d1.
38. Murray, B. (2018). Vietnam Is Winning the U.S.-China Trade War. *Foreign Policy.* https://foreignpolicy.com/2018/10/30/vietnam-is-winning-the-u-s-china-trade-war/.
39. Panda, A. (2019). With New South China Sea Tensions With Philippines, China Overplays Its Hand. *The Diplomat.* https://thediplomat.com/2019/04/with-new-philippine-tensions-china-overplays-its-hand/.
40. Pearson, J. & Gloystein, H. (2018). Vietnam halts South China Sea oil drilling project under pressure from Beijing. *Reuters.* https://www.reuters.com/article/us-southchinasea-vietnam-idUSKBN1GZ0JN.
41. Philstar.com. (2019). Vietnam rejects Beijing's South China Sea fishing ban that covers Philippine EEZ. Retrieved from https://www.philstar.com/headlines/2019/05/07/1915827/vietnam-rejects-beijings-south-china-sea-fishing-ban-covers-philippine-eez#MlmuAfh6rI72GWLu.99.
42. Rabena, A. J. (2018). Duterte's push for joint exploration in the South China Sea. *ASPI's The Strategist.* https://www.aspistrategist.org.au/dutertes-push-joint-exploration-south-china-sea/.
43. Reed, J. (2018). Dominant China pushes for oil and gas deals in Asia. *Financial Times.* https://www.ft.com/content/fbc10072-eece-11e8-89c8-d36339d835c0.
44. RFA Staff. (2019). Philippines: Duterte to Enforce Court Order to Protect South China Sea, Spokesman Says. *RFA.* https://www.rfa.org/english/news/china/philippines-southchinasea-05062019135345.html.
45. Rinen, F. C. (2019). PH, China see tourism as key player in poverty alleviation. *Philippine Information Agency* https://pia.gov.ph/news/articles/1022874.
46. Rosenberg, D. (Ed.). (2016). Introduction. *The South China Sea.* http://www.southchinasea.org/introduction/.
47. Scissors, D. (2020). China Global Investment Tracker. *American Enterprise Institute.* https://www.aei.org/china-global-investment-tracker/.
48. Sukumaran, T. (2019). China-Malaysia industrial park project draws US$4.8 billion in investments, fuelled partly by trade war. *South China Morning Post.* https://www.scmp.com/news/asia/southeast-asia/article/3014584/china-malaysia-industrial-park-project-draws-us48-billion.
49. Tadalan, C. A. (2019). Arroyo says China offers alternative development model. *Business World.* https://www.bworldonline.com/arroyo-says-china-offers-alternative-development-model/.
50. Torrecampo, R. C. (2019). It's Time to Rethink Philippine Policies on China. *The Diplomat.* https://thediplomat.com/2019/04/its-time-to-rethink-philippine-policies-on-china/.
51. Tran, K. K. (2015). *How will Vietnam's economic relationship and dependency on china affect its response to China's increasing threat to its*

sovereignty? Calhoun. https://calhoun.nps.edu/bitstream/handle/10945/45953/15Jun_Tran_Kevin.pdf?sequence=1&isAllowed=y.
52. Xinhua. (2019). Chinese tourists to Philippines increase nearly 25 pct in first three months of 2019. http://www.xinhuanet.com/english/2019-05/09/c_138046406.htm.
53. YingHui, L. (2018). China's Charm Offensive in the South China Sea. *Real Clear Defense.* https://www.realcleardefense.com/articles/2018/08/23/chinas_charm_offensive_in_the_south_china_sea_113726.html.

https://doi.org/10.1142/9781786349286_0003

Chapter 3

U.S.–China Rivalry and the Paradox of the South China Sea Disputes

David Rosenberg

For whosoever commands the sea commands the trade; whosoever commands the trade of the world commands the riches of the world, and consequently the world itself.

— Sir Walter Raleigh (1552–1618) [1]

3.1 Historical Background

The ocean enclosure movement started changing in the late 1700s when the United States of America became the first nation-state to extend its sovereign territory 3 miles offshore. Why 3 miles? U.S. Secretary of State Thomas Jefferson provided an answer for British authorities in 1793, in his statement, that the boundary of territorial waters of the new American republic was one sea league or three nautical miles, "the utmost range of a cannon ball."

The 3-mile "cannon-shot rule" remained in effect until 1945 when U.S. President Harry Truman issued a proclamation that the natural resources of the waters, the subsoil, and the seabed of the continental shelf adjacent to U.S. coasts are subject to U.S. jurisdiction and control. President Truman's decision was largely motivated by the discovery of offshore oil deposits and the anticipated surge in postwar energy demand.

Several countries followed the U.S. in extending their claims over offshore waters. In 1946, Argentina claimed control of its continental shelf and the sea above it. In 1947, Chile and Peru extended their jurisdiction to 200 miles offshore. In 1948, Iceland declared conservation zones beyond its 3-mile limit out to its continental shelf. In 1949, Iceland invoked a "headland to headland" rule. In 1950, Ecuador extended its jurisdiction to 200 miles. This process of creeping state jurisdiction continued around the oceans of the world.

Finally, in 1958, the United Nations convened a Conference on the Law of the Seas (UNCLOS) at Geneva, in an attempt to codify the proliferating claims. In 1974, the United Nations Conference on the Law of the Sea began talks on fisheries, navigation, seabed minerals, and pollution. By 1982, the talks produced a draft treaty for international ratification. It entered into force in 1994. As of 2018, 168 countries and the European Union have ratified the Convention.

3.2 UNCLOS and the Industrial Revolution of East Asia

UNCLOS provided a stable framework for the industrial revolution of East Asia. Japan, Hong Kong, Singapore, South Korea, Taiwan, Indonesia, Malaysia, Thailand, and China, since the 1980s, have all pursued export-led growth strategies during a fortuitous time. Tariffs and transportation costs were declining dramatically. Public investments in port facilities coincided with a big increase in the container shipping trade, especially in intermediate goods within the region. As a result, much of manufacturing moved from Europe and North America to East Asia. With the biggest and busiest container ports in the world, the South China Sea became the hub of the industrial revolution of East Asia. The standardization of the container unit, the automation of the loading and unloading process, and the careful coordination of ship, train, and truck movements greatly extended and accelerated supply chains to the mutual benefit of its participants [2].

The changes in distribution and cargo-handling capabilities of the world's biggest container ports show the major shifts that the world economy has undergone over the past two decades. The volume of cargo traded through the world's biggest container ports has increased vastly in the past 50 years. Five decades ago, more than half of the top 10 container

Table 3.1. Top 10 Container Ports of the World

	Port	Country	TEUs (000s)	Port	Country	TEUs (000s)
		1970			2017	
1	New York/NJ	U.S.A.	930	Shanghai	China	40,230
2	Oakland	U.S.A.	336	Singapore	Singapore	33,670
3	Rotterdam	Netherlands	242	Shenzhen	China	25,210
4	Seattle	U.S.A.	224	Ningbo	China	24,610
5	Antwerp	Belgium	215	Busan	South Korea	21,400
6	Belfast	N. Ireland	210	Hong Kong	SAR, China	20,760
7	Bremerhaven	Germany	195	Guangzhou	China	20,370
8	Los Angeles	U.S.A.	165	Qingdao	China	18,260
9	Melbourne	Australia	158	Dubai	UAE	15,440
10	Tilbury/London	UK	155	Tianjin	China	15,210

Source: https://en.wikipedia.org/wiki/List_of_busiest_container_ports.

ports were in America or Europe, reflecting imports into both regions from around the globe. Now, all but one of the top 10 container ports are in East Asia, with seven in China. Shanghai and Singapore are the two busiest container shipping ports in the world. Hong Kong and Ningbo are close behind (Table 3.1).

Today, most containers are carrying intermediate goods — often among subsidiaries of multinational corporations — that have been partially processed in one country in East Asia and will be further processed in another one in East Asia. The success of intraregional container shipping depends greatly on close cooperation of all participants, from policymakers to technical working groups to container handlers. Clearly, cooperation pays when it provides tangible mutual benefits.

By the end of the 20th century, the South China Sea had become the hub of the industrial revolution in Asia. China has now become the main engine of that economic growth. Every Asian country now trades more with China than with the United States, often by a margin of two to one. China is already central to global economic welfare and opportunity. It is the world's largest trading nation, the world's second-biggest economy, besides, it is also the world's biggest supplier of manufactured goods, and the world's biggest consumer of energy and a large range of industrial raw materials. China's economic activity impacts every aspect of global economic life. This gives China a substantial soft power advantage, especially in East Asia.

3.3 The Costs of Economic Growth

Rapid economic growth around the South China Sea has also led to growing problems, including resource depletion, pollution, poaching, illegal migration, piracy, and terrorism threats. The driving forces for these problems are increasing resource competition, resource nationalism, military modernization, and conflicting territorial claims. Resource competition is the result of deeply rooted, long-term trends of coastal urbanization, export-oriented industrialization, rising consumption, and the resulting competition for vital resources, especially fisheries and hydrocarbons.

Resource nationalism is strong in East Asia, where most states actively manage their economies to pursue their national agendas. Coastal states want to extend their sovereignty over the many islands and reefs in the South China Sea to anchor their claims for asserting an Exclusive Economic Zone (EEZ) up to 200 miles beyond their coastlines, as provided by UNCLOS, thereby gaining control over the fisheries and hydrocarbon resources they are thought to contain. This is further encouraged by opportunistic politicians and local authorities seeking to demonstrate their patriotism to protect national sovereignty and defend the homeland. This has been aggravated by episodes of xenophobia in domestic political activities during recent major leadership transitions in North Korea, South Korea, Japan, China, and other countries.

Military modernization programs have been pursued by several littoral countries. These developments in turn have aroused the concern of their neighbors, as well as commercial and naval stakeholders, who want to preserve the freedom of the seas, or provide unrestricted access to the seas and the straits of the South China Sea and its archipelagic waterways for their mercantile and naval vessels. The threat of a regional arms race has also been exacerbated by the seemingly intractable disputes over the numerous overlapping and conflicting territorial claims to the hundreds of small features in the South China Sea, including uninhabited islets, shoals, reefs, banks, sand bars, cays, and rocks. The dispute over the Spratly Islands involves as many as six parties (Mainland China, Taiwan, Malaysia, Vietnam, the Philippines, and Brunei), all of whom have made claims over the Spratly Islands, in whole or in part, and their surrounding water areas. Given the high degree of regional economic inter-dependence, it is not surprising there have been numerous incidents and conflicts, especially those involving survey vessels or fishing boats on the seas. However, there are few well-tested ways to resolve these low-level but frequent conflicts. Hence, there are likely to be more confrontations and conflicts ahead, unless better conflict management can be institutionalized.

3.4 China's Territorial Claims

The most controversial maritime territorial issue is China's 9-dash line claim to the South China Sea. The modern history of this line goes back to December 1914, when Hu Jinjie, a Chinese cartographer, published a map with a line around only the Pratas and Paracels, entitled "the Chinese territorial map before the Qianglong-Jiaqing period of the Qing Dynasty (AD 1736–1820)." In 1935, the Land and Water Maps Inspection Committee of the Republic of China (ROC) published a "Map of Chinese Islands in the South China Sea" with an 11-dotted line drawn around 132 islets and reefs of the four South China Sea archipelagos. In 1947, The ROC Ministry of Interior prepared a location map for internal use, renaming the islands in the South China Sea and formally allocating their administration to the Hainan Special Region. One year later, the Atlas of Administrative Areas of the Republic of China was officially published, including the first official map with the line for the South China Sea. An eleven-segment line was drawn instead of the previous continuous line. In 1949, the newly established People's Republic of China (PRC) published a "Map of China" with the eleven-dotted line. In 1953, after Premier Zhou Enlai's approval, the two-dotted line portion in the Gulf of Tonkin was deleted. Chinese maps published since 1953 have shown the nine-dotted line in the South China Sea.

In sum, the PRC inherited and maintained the claims first developed by the ROC, the predecessor of the current government, on Taiwan. Further, the current claims of the Beijing government and the Taiwan government are essentially the same. Indeed, the Taiwan government occupies the largest of the Spratly Islands, Itu Aba (Tai Ping Dao). The Beijing government and the Taipei government may disagree on many issues, but in the South China Sea, their claims are essentially the same. China's policy on settling maritime territorial disputes has gone through shifting patterns of cooperation and confrontation over the past decade. However, it became consistently more assertive in 2009 after Malaysia,

Vietnam, and the Philippines submitted their claims to the UN Commission on the Limits to the Continental Shelf (CLCS). The CLCS provides that if the coastal state can provide evidence that its continental shelf extends beyond 200 nautical miles, it can claim EEZ jurisdiction up to a limit of 350 miles beyond its coastline.

Malaysia and Vietnam submitted their claims on 6 May 2009. Vietnam submitted additional claims on 7 May 2009. The Philippines objected to these claims and made a partial submission of its own claims.

China then protested that these submissions seriously infringed China's sovereignty and jurisdiction in the South China Sea. In its protest note to the CLCS, China asserted that "China has indisputable sovereignty over the islands in the South China Sea and the adjacent waters and enjoys sovereign rights and jurisdiction over the relevant waters as well as the seabed and subsoil thereof (see Figure 3.1) — PRC Note Verbale, UN CLCSC, 7 May 2009."

The biggest controversy was caused by the attached map (see Figure 3.1). The claim and the attached map generated an outburst of diplomatic protest. Is China officially claiming all the waters within the u-shaped line as its territorial or historic waters? What is the basis for its "indisputable sovereignty"? What are the boundaries of "adjacent waters" and "relevant waters"? What exactly is an island? Many of the contested features are rocks or submerged shoals, not islands. According to Article 121 of the UNCLOS, features that "cannot sustain human habitation or economic life of their own" cannot have an EEZ or continental shelf of their own.

The issue was further complicated by China's new national map which re-affirms its historical South China Sea claims and incorporates a tenth "dash line" off Taiwan. Authorized by the State Bureau of Surveying and Mapping in June 2013, the 10-dash line map is also in the background in China's latest passports, which have drawn protests from Vietnam and the Philippines. In an article in the *American Journal of International Law*, Judge Gao Zhiguo, China's appointee to the International Tribunal for the Law of the Sea, said that the dashed line has three meanings: first, "it represents the title to the island groups that it encloses"; second, "it preserves Chinese historic rights in fishing, navigation, and such other marine activities as oil and gas development in the waters and on the continental shelf surrounded by the line"; and third, it may serve as a basis for "potential maritime delimitation lines" [6].

Figure 3.1. China's 9-Dash Line Map of South China Sea Claims

Source: South China Sea Virtual Library www.southchinasea.org.

3.5 Xi Jinping's Objectives

Xi Jinping presented several ambitious goals for China's future at the 19th Communist Party Congress in 2017. By 2021, the 100th anniversary of the Communist Party of China, he predicted that China would reach a per capita GDP of US$10,000. That seems possible, according to current forecasts. By 2035, China would become a "modern socialist country," implying a major reduction in poverty and pollution. By 2049, it would be a "fully developed nation," suggesting it would achieve an income per capita comparable to the OECD (Organization for Economic Co-operation and Development) median [5]. By 2050, China would become a "great power," often taken to mean reunification with Hong Kong and Taiwan.

In the South China Sea, Xi Jinping's strategy is to become more assertive in gaining control over the island groups within the 9-dash (now 10-dash) line, in preserving Chinese historic rights in fishing, navigation, and oil and gas development, and in providing a basis for potential maritime delimitation lines, while avoiding any adverse reaction from other coastal states or the U.S.

He has pursued four policies to achieve this. First, he seeks legitimacy for China's centuries-old historical rights in the region. The 2009 UN submission stating China's "indisputable sovereignty" announced this policy. This appears to be the first time China attached this map to an official communication to the UN.

Second, China is establishing new administrative authorities for maritime policy in the region. Sansha was designated as a prefecture-level city with control over the South China Sea in 2012. In January 2014, it established new fishing regulations, which oblige all foreign fishing vessels to apply for permission before entering a vast swath of the South China Sea, including areas contested by Vietnam and the Philippines.

Third, Chinese naval capabilities are being upgraded by re-organizing and arming maritime forces from the China Marine Surveillance and the Fishery Law Enforcement Command into a unified Coast Guard and a Maritime Militia. China has rapidly built extensive military bases and facilities on several reefs and shoals in the Spratly Islands. The Chinese Navy built a new base for its nuclear submarine fleet on Hainan Island.

Armed maritime patrol ships have been dispatched to prevent their fishermen from being arrested by foreign nations. China has used force and pre-emptive occupation to remove Vietnamese and Filipino vessels and forces from contested areas. In one highly publicized confrontation,

China stationed a giant oil drilling platform inside Vietnam's claimed EEZ in May 2014, supported by a large number of military vessels. The two governments traded accusations about the ramming of their boats. However, Vietnam pushed back forcefully. There were large anti-Chinese demonstrations in Vietnam and anti-Vietnamese demonstrations in China. Hundreds of expatriate workers were hurt. Thousands were evacuated home. Several Taiwanese as well as PRC businesses in Vietnam suffered heavy damage. China withdrew the oil rig and has not repeated the gambit.

Fourth, China is playing a selective but more active role in regional forums. For example, a naval code of conduct "for Unplanned Encounters at Sea" (CUES) was endorsed in April 2014 by naval officials from the United States, China, Japan, South Korea, Australia, and fifteen other states at the biennial Western Pacific Naval Symposium in Qingdao.

3.6 U.S. and P.R.C. Views on Maritime Law and National Sovereignty

What military activities are permissible in another country's EEZ in the South China Sea? How does the UNCLOS govern territorial claims in these waters? The UNCLOS authorizes coastal states to claim EEZs up to 200 nautical miles beyond their coastlines. They may exercise "sovereign rights and duties over living and non-living resources of the EEZ, and jurisdiction in relation to artificial islands, installations, and structures; marine scientific research (MSR); and the protection and preservation of the marine environment." Other states may use the EEZ, with "due regard" for the rights and duties of the coastal state. But the UNCLOS does not clearly define "due regard" or what constitutes permissible military activity or marine scientific research.

China, which has signed the UNCLOS treaty, maintains that military operations, hydrographic surveying, and intelligence collection by foreign ships or planes can be carried out in an EEZ only with permission from the coastal state. Although the U.S. has not signed the UNCLOS, it contends that collecting marine data for its own military purposes is permitted by the traditional freedom of navigation in international waters, including in the EEZ of another country without that country's consent. The United States, Japan, and other countries with major shipping and naval interests want to maintain freedom of navigation through the straits and sea lanes of the South China Sea for their oil tankers, container ships, and naval vessels. The U.S. sends its warships, including aircraft carriers from its Pacific Fleet, through the South China Sea in support of its military missions in the Arabian Sea and Persian Gulf. It is the vital artery that connects Japan with its Middle East energy suppliers.

There is general agreement that freedom of navigation in and above EEZs should not interfere with the rights of the coastal state. However, there is still disagreement about when these passages become intrusive eavesdropping missions to scout the defenses of potential rivals. The United States apparently will continue naval surveillance in the South China Sea, and China will continue to object to activities in disputed waters. Future confrontations between the U.S. and China in the South China Sea seem likely. The danger is that every incident is vulnerable to misinterpretation and has the potential to produce a far wider conflict.

In the short term, they are unlikely to escalate into a major conflict because there are more pressing priorities for Sino-American relations. The economies of the two countries are closely intertwined. U.S. corporations rely on China as a huge, cheap labor supply and China depends on the U.S. as a major market for its goods. China continues to buy U.S. Treasury bonds. The U.S., the world's biggest debtor, finds itself indebted to China, the world's biggest creditor. At the same, China depends heavily on access to U.S. technology and consumer markets for its continued economic growth. There have been serious confrontations such as the EP3 spy plane collision with a Chinese fighter jet in April 2001, the "cabbage tactics" of swarming Chinese maritime forces harassing the U.S. *Impeccable* in March 2009, and the People's Liberation Army Navy (PLAN) catch-and-release of a U.S. unmanned underwater vehicle (UUV) in December 2016. These confrontations have led to protests and demonstrations, but so far these have not led to the unravelling of the complex interdependence of Sino-American relations.

In the long term, China seems intent on extending its sphere of influence in East Asian seas, thereby eroding U.S. dominance and alliances in the region. This is a Chinese version of the Monroe Doctrine or the old Middle Kingdom order. In 1823, U.S. President James Monroe announced what came to be known as the Monroe Doctrine, stating that any further efforts by European powers to colonize or interfere with states in North or South America would be viewed as an act of aggression and require U.S. intervention. At the time, the United States had no significant navy, and Britain continued to act as it saw fit, especially in the Caribbean, a body of water that is as close and crucial to the United States as the South China Sea is to China. It took a few generations before the U.S. had a credible capability to enforce the doctrine.

There is a great irony in this: China's rise has been made possible because of the global trading system and alliances that Washington created after World War II. Until the recent Trump administration's tariff hikes, the U.S. had not prevented China from buying resources or exporting its goods. On the contrary, its navy had a stabilizing effect that made China's vast seaborne trade possible.

3.7 The U.S. Shift from Post-War International "Rules-Based Order" to Trump's New Nationalism

The United States has long viewed the South China Sea as an international waterway that allows "innocent passage" through its waters. During the Obama administration, the U.S. pursued a pivot or rebalance to Asia in economic and military terms: A Trans-Pacific Partnership, some naval re-positioning, and Freedom of Navigation Operations (FONOPs). It remained officially neutral on territorial disputes in the South China Sea. Its chief concerns were constraining North Korea's nuclear weapons development and deployment of its THAAD missile defense system in South Korea.

U.S. defense strategy under Obama was moving toward low-cost, low-risk operations, more dependent on increased financial support and logistical assistance from regional allies and partners. The U.S. then seemed unlikely to intervene militarily in any naval skirmish between China and other territorial claimants in the South China Sea. In response to China's increasing assertiveness, the U.S. increased its FONOP patrols there as well as military aid and joint naval exercises with coastal countries.

The Trump administration made some big changes. It still views the South China Sea as international waters and is increasing its freedom of navigation patrols. But Trump's "America First" policy challenged the long-term value of U.S. military and political alliances and partnerships. His global economic policy is protectionist and mercantilist. It and seeks to impose tariffs and restrictions on the open trade and investment system that has prevailed since the mid-1940s. The Trump administration initially called for "trade war" with China, claiming that "China is ripping off the U.S. on trade."

The U.S. Defense Department now views China as a "strategic competitor" or a "competitive rival" and a threat to U.S. power in the region [8]. Defense Secretary James Mattis said the U.S. needed to strengthen its competitive edge in air, land, sea, space, and cyberspace weapons systems, including nuclear weapons. In turn, U.S. President Trump requested an unprecedented 10% increase in defense spending. The U.S. approach now resembles the "peace through strength" policy of the Reagan era.

3.8 China's Maritime Gray Zone Operations: "Push, Push, But Don't Break"

China's main strategic interests in the South China Sea are, according to Jia Deng of Nanjing University, to counter-balance the U.S. influence, to gain access to the Pacific Ocean through the Miyoko Strait and the Bashi Strait (above and below Taiwan), and to become a maritime power to protect its vital interests. China argues that the South China Sea has historically been Chinese, and it is only defending what it views as its historic rights and interests in its territorial waters. It has been highly effective in changing the status quo in the East Asian seas without resorting to armed conflict or war, despite opposition from several coastal states and the U.S.

China is gaining substantial influence through gray zone operations, a comprehensive, long-term strategy that emphasizes the use of paramilitary forces — especially the China Coast Guard (CCG) and the People's Armed Forces Maritime Militia (PAFMM) — "on the frontlines of China's seaward expansion." They have been able to occupy natural and artificially created islands, develop military facilities, and pressure and intimidate rivals, while carefully avoiding any serious reaction from its main maritime rival, the U.S. It is a strategy of "Push, push, but don't break."

The term gray zone refers to maritime activities that are not clearly peacetime or wartime but are intentionally ambiguous to minimize the risk of precipitating an armed conflict. It should however be noted that gray zone is not the same as gray hull, the color of PLA Navy vessels. CCG vessel hulls are white, while PAFMM vessel hulls are blue. Gray zone operations seek to alter the status quo incrementally and gradually, by employing unconventional elements of state power; e.g., fishermen militias. PAFMM personnel are mostly civilian fishermen. But they can also be used to assert China's sovereignty claims and resource control. Some are trained and paid to do so, under a direct military chain of command of the PAFMM, a state-organized and controlled maritime force.

The CCG and the PAFMM carry out most of the Chinese maritime gray zone operations. Most CCG cutters and PAFMM vessels are minimally armed, but they can bump, ram, and obstruct other vessels. They can also employ powerful water cannons to damage sensitive equipment aboard other ships. They can maintain a Chinese presence in contested waters, thereby "declaring sovereignty." They can provide intelligence, surveillance, and reconnaissance. They can intimidate and harass foreign vessels found fishing or pursuing oil and gas development activities in disputed maritime space. They can protect Chinese civilians operating in Chinese-claimed maritime space; for example, in their defense of the Chinese drilling rig HYSY-981 in 2014 and in Chinese encroachment over Scarborough Reef, a feature clearly within the Philippines' EEZ. The PLA Navy also plays a role in disputed waters, by hovering nearby to discourage foreign countries from any forceful resistance to Chinese activities.

The Chinese encroachment at Scarborough Shoal is a notable example of its maritime gray zone operations to change the status quo in the South China Sea. The confrontation began in April 2012 when a Philippine Navy vessel attempted to detain eight Chinese fishing boats that had entered waters around Scarborough Shoal, claimed by both China and the Philippines. An armed boarding party from the Philippine frigate discovered that the fishing boats were in possession of a large illegal catch of coral, giant clams, sea turtles, and live sharks. Two Chinese surveillance vessels blocked the frigate from pursuing any further action. Foreign affairs officials in the Philippines and China were consulted and they agreed to negotiate a non-violent, diplomatic end to the confrontation. But both sides insisted that they would defend their territorial claims. All of the Chinese fishing boats left the shoal unhindered, with their illegal catch. Philippine vessels left the area to avoid a threatening typhoon. Chinese coast guard patrol boats remained. They have now effectively occupied the shoal.

The Philippine government protested that, according to the UNCLOS, Scarborough Shoal is clearly within its EEZ. It tried to get support from ASEAN to restrain Chinese actions, without much success. It sought and received some support from the U.S. to improve its maritime surveillance and patrol capabilities. The Philippines finally took China to court to protest its occupation of Scarborough Shoal by appealing to an international tribunal at the Permanent Court of Arbitration (PCA) at The Hague. In its legal suit, the Philippine government was careful to avoid the issue of sovereignty claims. It sought an opinion on whether these features were islands, rocks, or submerged shoals.

On July 12, 2016, the PCA ruled that UNCLOS supersedes any historical claims by China or Taiwan. It also ruled that none of the rocks, shoals, or low-tide elevations in the Spratlys were islands and could not generate any EEZ or continental shelf claims. It also said that China's artificial island construction was unwarranted and in violation of UNCLOS environmental provisions.

The tribunal's rulings were final and binding. The PCA had no enforcement authority or capability, but its rulings have been endorsed by all other claimant states. However, China refused to acknowledge or accept the tribunal's jurisdiction or its decision. The Aquino administration endorsed the PCA rulings on Philippine sovereignty over islands in the South China Sea. But in December 2016, Philippine President Duterte said he would set aside the PCA ruling in the interests of better relations with China. Today, Filipino fishermen can only operate there with China's permission.

China's sweeping sovereignty claims have been substantially weakened by the PCA ruling. China was well aware of UNCLOS guidelines for negotiating maritime boundaries as it had already done so in the 2004 Sino-Vietnamese Agreements on boundary delimitation and joint fisheries management in the Tonkin Gulf. This is the one — and so far, the only — case where China has successfully negotiated, bargained, and compromised over a maritime boundary dispute, by following the guidelines provided by UNCLOS.

China continues to assert a manifestly ambiguous historical claim to most of the South China Sea. However, recent historical work on China's claims to the South China Sea finds that China's claims are not ancient, but quite modern. For example, the first known claim to James Shoal, the southernmost feature within the 9-dash line, did not appear until 1936. They developed in response to domestic political crises among contending factions in China in the 1920s and 1930s, a time of rising nationalist sentiments [4]. Despite the legal precedents and historical evidence, China now apparently pursues a policy of "might makes right." The PLA Navy, the CCG, and the PAFMM are now the largest of their type in the world, in terms of number of vessels. To support their operation, China has made an extraordinarily rapid and extensive effort to build artificial islands and military facilities in disputed waters of the South China Sea.

China now has by far the world's largest coast guard, operating more maritime law enforcement vessels than the coast guards of all its regional neighbors combined. The CCG owns more than 220 ships over 500 tons, far surpassing Japan (with around 80 coast guard hulls over 500 tons), the United States (with around 50), and South Korea (with around 45). The size of the PAFMM is difficult to determine. However, it recruits from the world's largest fishing industry, with nearly two million fishermen operating about 187,000 marine fishing vessels.

There have been diverse responses from regional states to Chinese encroachments. Japan has taken the most vigorous actions by strengthening its naval and coast guard forces along its southern islands. Vietnam has resisted Chinese claims and activities in contested fishing and oil exploration areas, but with only mixed results. The Philippines is apparently acquiescing to Beijing control over Scarborough Shoal, despite a 2016 arbitration ruling clearly placing it under Philippine jurisdiction. China has exercised restraint in its confrontation with the Philippines over Scarborough Shoal, especially with President Duterte, according to China scholar Jia Deng. The CCP gets a lot of domestic pressure to resist encroachment by other countries. China prefers pragmatic cooperation and quiet, bilateral diplomacy to settle disputes. China's gray zone operations affect U.S. interests directly and indirectly. U.S. efforts to defend its own interests of maritime freedom in the East Asian seas have been fairly successful. Nevertheless, several U.S. Navy special mission ships — the USNS *Bowditch*, USNS *Impeccable*, USNS *Effective*, USNS *Victorious*, and USNS *Howard O. Lorenzen* — have all been shadowed and harassed by various Chinese maritime forces demonstrating their opposition to foreign naval activities within its claimed EEZ.

When it comes to indirect effects, the United States has a mixed record of helping its allies and partners protect themselves against Chinese intrusion. Despite the robust presence of American sea power in contested areas of maritime East Asia and despite the periodic FONOPs, the United States has largely failed to halt China's bullying behavior against its smaller neighbors. The former (presence) cannot deter Beijing from taking tactical actions in the gray zone. The latter (FONOPs) do little to defend the interests of allies and partners. China's gray zone activities cannot be easily deterred, because each individual act is calculated to fall below the U.S. escalation threshold to a more forceful retaliation.

How could the U.S. pursue more effective ways to constrain China's maritime intrusions and manage confrontations when they do occur? With its allies and partners, the U.S. could increase surface and satellite surveillance of maritime hotspots. It could expand the Shiprider Program and other forms of joint or coordinated patrols and exercises, publicize and protest all acts of Chinese encroachment and militarization swiftly and widely, and escort allied vessels through contested waters or help allies protect their own EEZs from Chinese intrusions. All these options imply a lower threshold for U.S. retaliation along with acceptance of a higher risk of escalation. China does not want war but will continue pursuing maritime expansion opportunistically until it encounters stiffer resistance. Until China has its own credible capability to enforce its doctrine, it will pursue its claims in maritime East Asia through its incremental policy of "reactive assertiveness," "tailored coercion," or "forceful persuasion." [10] Perhaps the U.S. and its allies and partners should deploy their own gray zone forces.

3.9 ASEAN's Role

ASEAN would seem to be a suitable venue for dispute settlement. However, there are major differences among ASEAN members in terms of their history, culture, natural resource endowments, and strategic priorities and capabilities. They disagree on basic economic and security issues, including how to deal with the U.S. and with China. Several littoral states (Brunei, Singapore, and Malaysia) support the U.S.-initiated Trans-Pacific Partnership, which excludes China. The mainland ASEAN states (Cambodia, Laos, Myanmar, and Thailand) support the China-initiated Regional Comprehensive Economic Partnership, which excludes the U.S.

With regard to territorial disputes in the South China Sea, Cambodia actively supports China's policy against internationalizing the issue; i.e., not involving the U.S. or any international agencies in dispute settlement. The other mainland states — Laos, Myanmar, and Thailand — maintain a low-profile role but generally defer to China's preferences.

The four states that have conflicting claims with China — The Philippines, Vietnam, Malaysia, and Brunei — are themselves internally divided. The Vietnamese and Philippine governments have both sought some outside support from UNCLOS, from the U.S., and from Japan to resist the continued pressure from China and Taiwan to assert their claims in the South China Sea. The Philippine government has appealed to the UNCLOS Arbitration Tribunal for a ruling on the status of Scarborough Shoal, and thereby challenge China's occupation. Malaysia and Brunei avoid public criticism of China's claims but do support finding a unified ASEAN position on the disputes. Indonesia and Singapore have no conflicting claims with China. They are both strong advocates of maritime security and freedom of navigation, a position shared by the U.S. Additional efforts by all interested parties will be necessary to get China and Taiwan to clarify the delineation of the 9-dash line, and bring it under the jurisdiction of dispute settlement mechanisms under UNCLOS and other courts.

In the absence of any widely-agreed-upon and well-tested way to determine how to govern the resources of the South China Sea, countries have occupied features and based their claims on different standards of evaluation. For example, China and Taiwan invoke the standard of historical usage and occupation. Malaysia and Vietnam base some of their claims on the continental shelf extension of their national territory. The Philippines invokes the legal provisions of UNCLOS. The territorial disputes over maritime boundaries are complex and unlikely to be resolved in the foreseeable future. In the meantime, fish stocks are being depleted due to overfishing, marine habitats are being destroyed, good order at sea is lacking, and there is inadequate marine scientific knowledge to provide for the development of its resources.

The coastal states of the South China Sea or ASEAN have failed to create an effective maritime security institution on their own. The U.S. has been unsuccessful in its efforts to form an ad hoc coalition of Southeast Asian countries that might constrain China's ambitions in the South China Sea. It should be noted that Cambodia, Indonesia, Malaysia, the Philippines, Thailand, and Vietnam have all claimed restrictions on the freedoms of navigation similar to those imposed by China. ASEAN, the Association of Southeast Asian Nations, has so far been unable to form a common position for dealing with China or Taiwan on these issues.

In order to prevent acquiescence to China's claims over the Spratly islands, a concerted, multilateral effort is needed. The U.S. will have to use its soft power to create networks and institutions that will allow it to cooperate with China, India, Japan, Europe, and others to deal with transnational problems — for example, monetary stability, climate change, terrorism, and cybercrime — that no country can solve unilaterally. That will require overcoming the unilateral policies and attitudes associated with the Trump administration.

The U.S., Japan, S. Korea, India, Australia, and other like-minded navies, either singly or jointly, could continue to assert traditional freedom of navigation by sailing through and flying over the South China Sea where international law allows and either rebuff or ignore China's pretentious objections. This would require a sustained diplomatic effort, something the U.S. is currently unwilling and under-staffed to do. As of March 2018, the Trump administration had appointed only 70 of 188 U.S. ambassadors. At the same time, it had increased the deployment of special operations forces to 149 countries — up from 138 during the Obama administration in 2016. U.S. ambassadors are operating in one-third of the world's capitals, and special operations forces are active in three-fourths [9]. Additional efforts by all interested parties will be necessary to get China and Taiwan to clarify the delineation of the 9-dash or 10-dash line and bring it under the jurisdiction of dispute settlement mechanisms under UNCLOS and other courts.

3.10 Conclusions

3.10.1 *China's dilemma: International law or international outlaw?*

China faces a dilemma. On the one hand, it wants to continue expanding its influence in the South China Sea despite the legal rulings and constraints of UNCLOS. On the other hand, it needs to demonstrate its commitment to the rule of law to gain support for its major initiatives such as the Asian Infrastructure Investment Bank (AIIB), the Belt and Road Initiative (BRI), and the Regional Comprehensive Economic Partnership (RCEP). If China disregards the tribunal's decision, it risks being branded an international outlaw. It might drive regional states closer to Tokyo and Washington. These costs to Beijing could make an eventual political compromise more appealing. China might agree to clarify and redefine the "9-dash line" based on UNCLOS rather than historic rights and enter into real negotiations with its neighbors.

Is this the beginning of another Cold War? There are some similarities. Both China and the U.S. are now conducting increased air and sea patrols and exercises in the region to exhibit their strength, capacity, and preparedness. This rivalry puts pressure on countries around the South

China Sea to take sides. Alliances and partnerships are being pursued to seek an advantage in the regional balance of power. However, there has not been any polarizing trends toward opposing forces like the post-war NATO and Warsaw Pact military alliances. Despite the "war of words," neither side appears to want an armed conflict. However, as more combat ships and aircraft are added in a relatively small maritime space, the possibility of military encounters and/or accidents is increasing. The risk is increased when states or their navies support their fishermen, even when they are fishing illegally or poaching. Arming marine police boats blurs the distinction between traditional and non-traditional security concerns and further increases the risk that inadvertent incidents might escalate into a violent conflict.

3.10.2 *An emerging concert of powers?*

Despite the tit-for-tat tariff hikes between China and the U.S., the driving forces in the current global power balance shift are not primarily economic. They are political, especially the changes in long-term strategic vision in the U.S. (more insular) and China (more regional). China is pursuing a larger role in the world while the U.S. is pursuing a smaller one. This is what explains the power balance shifts from the period of bipolar balance (the U.S. and the U.S.S.R., 1946–1989/92) to a unipolar balance (U.S., 1989/92–2001) to a multi-polar (2001–present). The multi-polar powers now include the U.S., the E.U., Russia, Japan, China, and India. They may constitute a new "concert of powers." There are, of course, many obstacles to overcome in establishing a new Concert of Powers. There are more second-tier powers to contend with: Pakistan, Mexico, Brazil, Turkey, Iran, and perhaps others. A bipolar balance of alliances may evolve between the nascent Shanghai Cooperation Organization (Russia & China) and the Indo-Pacific Security Dialogue (U.S., Japan, Australia, India, and sometimes Taiwan).

We might also be moving toward an "age of non-polarity," as Richard Haass describes it, in which nationalist powers — China, the U.S., and Russia — contend with diverse non-state groups, from Doctors Without Borders to Facebook, and ExxonMobil to Boko Haram [7]. Ironically, in both China and the United States, people who are infuriated by profound gaps in wealth and opportunity have pinned their hopes on nationalist, nostalgic leaders, who encourage them to imagine threats from the outside world. They are all trying to be great again.

3.10.3 *Provisional solutions for persistent problems*

Even in the absence of a widely accepted and effective regional security system, there are some things that can be done to improve resource sharing and maritime security in the South China Sea. It has happened before, as evidenced in the 2004 Sino-Vietnamese Tonkin Gulf agreements on boundary delimitation and joint fisheries management, CCSBT (the Commission for the Conservation of Southern Bluefin Tuna), STRAITREP, (Ship Traffic Management System in the Straits of Malacca and Singapore), naval hotlines, anti-piracy programs, and numerous other bilateral and multilateral agreements.

One good possibility would be to extend the existing Tonkin Gulf agreement. In a February 2016 meeting in Hanoi, Vietnamese and Chinese working group experts discussed ways to extend the delimitation of the sea area adjacent to the Tonkin Gulf. They agreed on a joint research program for the conservation of marine life and island environments in the Gulf of Tonkin and also on a research project on sedimentation in the Red River Delta. They proposed to continue their discussion on coordinating search and rescue (SAR) efforts at upcoming rounds of expert-level negotiations. These efforts should be continued.

A second option is for Southeast Asian coastal countries to explore negotiations with China for establishing joint fishery management zones in areas on the periphery of the "9-dash line" where it overlaps with EEZs of other countries. These tend to be relatively small areas in relatively remote locations. Ten agreements have been negotiated so far among seven coastal countries since 1969. Many more are currently under negotiation.

A third option is to take China at its word when it calls for maritime cooperation. For example, at the 2015 Boao Forum for Asia, Beijing officially launched the Year of ASEAN–China Maritime Cooperation. It announced that China and ASEAN nations would carry out cooperation in several areas of marine economy. Policymakers could work vigorously to test China's intentions and turn their pledges into targets and timetables. For example, technical working groups could be established to survey the scope and status of fishery resources in high-priority areas such as spawning grounds in the Coral Triangle.

As the world's largest producer and consumer of fish, China had a big stake in sustainable fishery management. Without joint management of common fisheries, irreversible and widespread damage to fish stocks is more likely. In the worst case, it may result in a fishery collapse similar to the tragedy of the commons in the North Atlantic cod fisheries in the 1990s.

A fourth option is to expand or emulate existing multilateral agreements, such as the Regional Cooperation Agreement on Combating Piracy and Armed Robbery against Ships in Asia (ReCAAP), the Malacca Strait navigation control system (STRAITREP), or the Code for Unplanned Encounters at Sea (CUES).

The extensive naval modernization programs in the region are not inherently threatening, but can become so without more confidence-building measures, such as hotlines and military-to-military contacts, including joint patrols and exercises. An "incidents at sea" agreement could provide a hotline or emergency response system to report confrontations involving fishing vessel seizures and crew detentions.

Another possibility is to explore Taiwan's growing interest in maritime cooperation. Taiwan's Environmental Protection Administration had proposed expanding its program to monitor environmental quality around Itu Aba Island into a multilateral effort covering the Spratly Islands. It had also proposed setting aside ecologically valuable areas for protected marine reserves. In both of the above cases, multilateral cooperation may facilitate at least provisional boundary delimitation for environmental protection and resource management.

There are also some intrinsically global problems that require cooperation and hence the motivation to overcome all these obstacles to find effective solutions. These include global climate change, Jihadist terrorism, epidemics, economic inequalities, and migration. As one authoritative analysis concludes, "ultimately, the goal is to pressure China to recognize that its interests would be better served by a more cooperative approach." [3]

References

1. Raleigh, W. (1965). *The Works of Sir Walter Ralegh, Kt.: Now First Collected, to Which is Prefixed: The Lives of the Author*. New York: Burt Franklin.
2. Demil, B. & Lecocq, X. (2006). *The Tin Can That Changed the World: The Institutionalization of Containerization*. Princeton University Press.
3. Erickson, A. S., Hickey, J., Holst, H., & Martinson, R. D. (2019). In A. S. Erickson & R. D. Martinson (Eds.), *China's Maritime Gray Zone*

Operations — 7th volume "Studies in Chinese maritime development" series. Naval Institute Press.
4. Hayton, B. (2015). *The South China Sea the Struggle for Power in Asia.* New Haven: Yale University Press.
5. Editorial Board. (2018). *Xi's new power and China's economic and social goals.* East Asia Forum. https://www.eastasiaforum.org/2018/03/19/xis-new-power-and-chinas-economic-and-social-goals/.
6. Graham, E. (2013). *China's new map: just another dash?* ASPI's The Strategist. http://www.aspistrategist.org.au/chinas-new-map-just-another-dash/.
7. Haass, R. N. (2008). The Age of Nonpolarity. *Foreign Affairs.* https://www.foreignaffairs.com/articles/united-states/2008-05-03/age-nonpolarity.
8. Mattis, J. (2018). Summary of the 2018 National Defense Strategy of The United States of America. https://www.dod.defense.gov/Portals/1/Documents/pubs/2018-National-Defense-Strategy-Summary.pdf.
9. Toft, M. D. (2018). *Fewer diplomats, more armed force defines US leadership today.* The Conversation. https://www.theconversation.com/fewer-diplomats-more-armed-force-defines-us-leadership-today-92890.
10. Yoon, S. (2014). Xi Jinping's "Monroe Doctrine": Rebuilding the Middle Kingdom Order? *RSIS Commentaries,* 102. RSIS. https://www.css.ethz.ch/en/services/digital-library/publications/publication.html/180601.

https://doi.org/10.1142/9781786349286_0004

Chapter 4

China's Relations with the Philippines Since Duterte: Challenges and Opportunities

Christopher B. Primiano

4.1 Introduction

China's actions in the South China Sea (SCS) have received significant attention in recent years, with escalating tensions and conflicts between China and other states. Using the 9-dash line as a basis for its claims, China has stated that the entire SCS belongs to China. In this context, numerous scholars, e.g., Hughes [14], Zhao [23], Callahan [3], and Yahuda [21], have argued that since the financial crisis of 2008, China has become more assertive, especially with the recent building of artificial islands for the ostensible purpose of projecting military force. In addition, observers have argued that in many instances China has refused to stand down regarding claims in the regional sea. This was best exemplified by its position against the 2016 pro-Philippines ruling of the International Tribunal at The Hague regarding China's claims to the SCS. Relations between China and the Philippines, however, improved dramatically shortly after Duterte became president.

In this chapter, I examine why China was willing to improve relations with the Philippines once Duterte became president and what that tells us about Chinese foreign policy. Moreover, I consider the larger picture of events in the South China Sea. China's relations with the Philippines needs to be placed in the context of broader Chinese foreign policy, especially its relations with the U.S., the U.S. military presence in the region, and China's main goal of advancing its version of global order.

The rest of the chapter consists of four sections. In section one, I provide background information and a literature review on China's actions in the SCS and International Relations (IR) theories to contextualize the chapter's focus. Section two traces and examines how the bilateral relationship between China and Philippines has evolved from the Aquino administration in 2012 to the present. That section analyzes the historical relations in three stages — (1) Tensions (the Aquino presidency 2010–2016), (2) Thawing relations (June 2016–March 2017), and (3) China asserts its control over the sea (starting in mid-March 2017) — to tease out the evolving foreign policy between the different leaders and periods. Section three analyzes the case and the broader implications. Then, in the last section, I offer a conclusion.

4.2 Background and IR Literature Review

4.2.1 *Chinese assertiveness*

Numerous scholars [2, 3, 14, 21, 23] have argued that due to the financial crisis in 2008, there has been a significant shift in Chinese foreign policy, pivoting toward a more assertive direction. Regarding the South China Sea in particular, numerous scholars have argued that such Chinese assertiveness has been clearly demonstrated e.g., Burgess [1], Cruz De Castro [6], Masuda [41], Friedberg [9], Brady [29], Zhao [23], and Yahuda [21]. According to Hughes [14], U.S. relations with China's neighboring countries, such as Japan, South Korea, and Vietnam, have improved as a direct outcome of such Chinese assertiveness. Yahuda [21] argues the main reason for such a change in Chinese assertiveness in the SCS was that with the financial crisis the Chinese government viewed U.S. power as descending and Chinese power as ascending. China's island building in the SCS and military installations on such islands demonstrate such assertiveness and raise serious concerns about China's military ambitions. The Chinese navy's use of water cannons in the SCS on Filipino fishermen advance Cruz De Castro's argument that the Chinese government has used "bullying tactics" in the SCS to advance China's maritime claims [6]. Friedberg provides the following assessment of China's actions regarding territorial disputes in the SCS: "In recent years, Beijing has repeatedly chosen to escalate ongoing disputes rather than wind them down." [9] As a result of such Chinese actions, numerous ASEAN states have been very concerned about a rising China [4, 18] and have sought anti-access/area denial (A2/AD) military capabilities [16].

Regarding Chinese assertiveness, scholars such as Moore [47], Yan [22], Chang-Liao [5], Masuda [41], and Hu [13] have argued that Xi Jinping has broken with Deng's *taoguangyanghui,* or keeping a low profile. Xi's speech on October 24, 2013 at the CCP's foreign affairs conference articulated his break from Deng's keeping a low profile by stating "*fenfayouwei*," which can be translated as striving for achievements [22]. At the nineteenth Party Congress in November 2017, Xi stated that time has come for China to be a more significant player in the world. This stated desire to advance China as a leading country in the world, in addition to limiting the U.S. presence in East Asia, needs to be considered when examining why China's relations with the Philippines changed.

4.2.2 *Realism*

According to realists, security is central for why states act the way they do. In particular, both the realist emphasis that states form alliances due to convenience and how states act to advance military power is applicable to China's actions in the case examined here, as China is interested in working with Duterte due to the larger aim of limiting the U.S. military in the region. Modifying Stephen Walt's balance of threat perception is useful for the case of China's relations with the Philippines. Defensive realist Stephen Walt posits that states balance against states that pose a threat to them [19]. While the Philippines was clearly not a threat to China in terms of a potential attack, nonetheless, the Philippines under Aquino III sided with the U.S. in an attempt to hinder China, which China viewed as a country thwarting its advancement and instead siding with the most powerful state in the world. For realism, capabilities explain why states act, as powerful states and weak states have different capabilities and thus act differently based on such capabilities [24]. This has been manifested in China's actions in the SCS with its assertiveness. Decades ago, China was not in the position of strength to assert itself as it has done recently. Thus, as China has increased its power, we have witnessed China doing more in the SCS, such as island building.

4.2.3 *Constructivism*

Constructivism emphasizes culture, history, values, identity, and social interactions. For constructivism, identity is essential in explaining why states act. Regarding the topic of respect, which is stressed in the constructivist literature, being respected or getting face plays a prominent role in Chinese society. In applying this to the international level, there are ample cases in which the Chinese government has been explicit that it either wants to be respected or is upset that it has not been respected.[a] Further demonstrating the importance that China places on its views of being respected, Kreuzer [15] argues that if the countries that China is competing with regarding territory and maritime issues in the SCS demonstrate that they recognize China's views (as Malaysia has done), or if such states are able to demonstrate that they are not threatening to China (also as Malaysia has done), then that will be well received by Beijing, and China will use restraint with such countries [15]. For Kreuzer, if countries choose to test China (as the Philippines has under Aquino), then China will be aggressive with such countries [15].[b] On the topic of being respected and deferred to, if actors are respected, then the chances for

[a]After the 2008 Olympic torch relay incident in France, in which there were anti-China protests and a protestor attempted to take the torch from a Chinese Paralympian, relations between France and China quickly inflamed. Due to the downturn in relations, President Sarkozy decided to issue an apology letter to China on behalf of France, which was widely circulated in China at the time. In that letter, Sarkozy stated: "I understand that the Chinese people's feelings were hurt by what went on that day, and especially by the intolerable attack you suffered and which I condemn with the utmost force." After receiving such face from a leader of a major Western power, the Chinese government was then willing to move beyond the previously mentioned event [for this case, see 49]. Relatedly, Moore argues that Chinese leaders want other states to show China much respect in world affairs, especially from states that are not as powerful as China [47].

[b]Since I limit the focus here to the PRC viewpoint of the relationship, see the following articles that devote attention to the Filipino side of the bilateral relationship. For an in-depth view on Duterte (e.g., the view that Duterte has long been anti-American, Duterte wants economic gains from China, he did not like U.S. criticism of his war on drugs, and how he views U.S. as an unreliable partner), see Murphy [17]. See Cruz De Castro [6] for how neorealism explains Aquino's reaction to China's actions in the SCS and see Cruz De Castro [7] for how Duterte wants economic gains from China on the one hand and on the other is balancing against China with developing relations with Japan. See Heydarian [12] for the role that domestic politics plays for Duterte's foreign policy.

cooperation are greater than if disrespected [20]. Being disrespected is likely to result in the actor being angry and not content, and thus the desire to redeem oneself for being treated accordingly [20].

This chapter thus combines aspects from both realism (e.g., China's quest for military power in the South China Sea) and constructivism (e.g., Chinese identity issues) in accounting for China's actions with the Philippines under Duterte.

4.3 Combined Bilateral Relations between China and the Philippines

This chapter has broadly categorized the bilateral engagement between China and the Philippines into three categories: (1) tension, (2) thawing relations, and (3) China asserts its control over the sea.

4.3.1 *Stage 1: Tensions (Aquino presidency)*

When Aquino was president of the Philippines, China and the Philippines had tense relations due to various factors — e.g., the Aquino administration had close ties with the U.S., did not engage in bilateral talks with Beijing regarding the SCS, and sought to use both regional and international organizations, such as ASEAN and the UN's International Tribunal at The Hague, as leverage with China regarding SCS issues [30]. Due to the Chinese desire to limit the U.S. presence in the region, the Chinese government did not want the president of the Philippines working closely with the U.S. in aiming to limit China in the region. Aquino, in short, was balancing against China and siding with the U.S. For those reasons, China viewed the Aquino administration as uncooperative, which had a negative impact on bilateral relations overall.

It was in that tense context that on January 23, 2013 the Aquino government brought their case to the Permanent Court of Arbitration regarding China's 9-dash line of the SCS and its territorial claims [53].[c] After three years of deliberation, the court rejected China's 9-dash line. Furthermore, the court also ruled that China violated Philippine access to fishing [40], supporting the Aquino government's claim. Even though

[c] China's 9-dash line used to be an eleven-dash line by the KMT in mainland China shortly after WWII [32].

China ratified the UN Convention on the Law of the Sea (UNCLOS), and by doing so China committed itself on paper to the international rules, China did not accept the ruling. In fact, China stated from the very beginning of the case that it will reject the tribunal's decision on this issue. Following that position, China refused to participate in the case when it was being heard by the court [53]. After the court's ruling, Beijing categorically rejected the court's ruling.[d]

During a Chinese government press conference in May 2015, China's foreign ministry spokesperson, Hua Chunying, stated, in a response to a question about the Philippines' criticism about Chinese island building/land reclamation, "China's sovereignty over the Nansha Islands and their adjacent waters is fully supported by historical and jurisprudential evidence." [35] Hua went on to add that the *Nansha* Islands have never belonged to the Philippines and depicted China's actions with such construction of the islands in a peaceful and productive way — "to better fulfill China's international responsibility and obligation in maritime search and rescue, navigation safety, ocean science and research, etc." In June of 2016, the month prior to the international court's ruling, China asserted its protest against the position of not just the Philippines, but also Japan and the U.S., by engaging in a joint naval exercise with Russia in which both countries sent ships near the *Diaoyu/Senkaku* Islands. Moreover, the joint exercise illustrates the comments from China's Ministry of National Defense spokesman that China and Russia were aiming to advance their military cooperation due to what they view as challenges in the SCS [18, 34]. In other words, China is not content with the U.S. military dominance in the Pacific region, as many countries in the region (e.g., South Korea, Japan, Vietnam, and Singapore) have military ties with the U.S. The issue of the U.S. military presence in the region is of great concern to China, and this needs to be considered when analyzing why China has changed its relations with the Philippines since Duterte. Given the tense relations that Russia had with the U.S. at the time of the naval exercise, China signaled to the U.S. that it was willing to conduct such a joint naval exercise with a leading U.S. adversary in the SCS to assert its view that it also seeks a strong military role in the SCS.[e]

---

[d] Writing shortly before the court's ruling, Graham Allison argued that if China disregarded the decision, it would be acting in a similar way with other great powers [26].

[e] Putin publicly stated his support for China against the international court's ruling regarding the SCS [39].

Then, in September of 2016, Russia and China conducted yet another naval exercise in the SCS [39].

China's desire to exert its military influence in the region has changed dramatically from the previous decades, due to the increased power that China has acquired in recent years, especially in the post-financial crisis years. Because Chinese economic and military capabilities have improved significantly, and the Chinese government has acted to advance itself accordingly. This demonstrates how, as observed in the previous section, Deng Xiaoping's advice of *taoguangyangui*, or keeping a low profile, is a thing of the past. When Deng was the leader of the country, China was not the economic or military power that it is today, and thus China needed to proceed with caution to achieve its primary goal of economic development. Since 2008, however, things have changed. Specifically, in the Xi era, in contrast to China of the 1980s and 1990s, China has sought to advance itself by Xi's stated goal of striving for achievements.

4.3.2 *Stage 2: Thawing relations (June 2016–March 2017)*

When campaigning for the presidency of his country, Duterte stated that he wanted bilateral talks with Beijing regarding the SCS. As argued above, since the Chinese government is focused on limiting the U.S. in the region, such a statement from a presidential contender is exactly the kind of partner China wants. After Duterte won the election on May 30, 2016, Xi sent Duterte a message to congratulate him ["Xi Jinping Sends Message," May 30, 2016], with the ostensible goal being to advance the spirit of cooperation and thus limit the U.S. in the region. Duterte, in keeping with his campaign pledge, upon winning the election but before being sworn in as president, held meetings with Chinese officials to chart a path of cooperation with China. Seeking to capitalize on what could be an improvement in relations, Xi, on Duterte's inauguration day, June 30, 2016, sent Duterte a message to congratulate him on becoming president of the Philippines [42]. Then, in August, Fidel Ramos, the former president of the Philippines, at Duterte's request, traveled to Hong Kong in an attempt to improve contacts with mainland China officials.

When Chinese Premier Li Keqiang spoke with Duterte on September 7, 2016, Duterte told Li that he wanted to have positive relations with China [46]. During that month, Duterte also stated that he wanted to advance ties with Russia [37]. Duterte's views on an alter-Western world or having power removed from the U.S. is precisely what China seeks in world politics, as its creation of the Asia Infrastructure Investment Bank, island building, and the China Dream demonstrate. The warming up of China–Philippines relations was demonstrated during Duterte's four-day state visit to China in October of 2016.[f] This visit was considered a game changer for Beijing–Manila relations. During that visit, Duterte publicly stated the distance that he wanted his country to have with the U.S. Duterte's stated position on not having a close relationship with the U.S. is reassuring to China, as China seeks to have more removed from the U.S. and Duterte will not seek U.S. support to go against China.

Soon after Duterte's visit, China's foreign ministry spokesperson, Hua Chunying, issued a statement: "We have seen all-round improvement of China-Philippines relations following President Duterte's visit to China. Under such circumstances, the Chinese side makes proper arrangements based on the friendship between China and the Philippines in response to the issue of President Duterte's concern" [45, 48]. Although the Chinese government statement highlighted how relations have improved between the two countries, and thus China is willing to work with the Philippines as a result of that, there was no mention about how China is benefitting from Duterte turning his back on the U.S. and embracing China. China, in short, is willing to work with Duterte due to strategic calculations related to security, despite the official government statement not saying anything about that. At face value, the impression that the government statement gives is that the Chinese government places much emphasis on the respect (or "friendship" to quote the spokesperson) that it is given in international relations. While being treated with respect is indeed important for China in international politics, the Philippines' shifting relations with the U.S. or the desire of Duterte to advance a world in which power is taken away from the U.S. is the main component for the turn-around in China–Philippines relations.

In late October 2016, with the improvement in relations, China acquiesced be allowing Filipino fishermen access to fish at the Scarborough Shoal, making it the first time since 2012 that the Philippines had access to fish there [33, 49].[g] The Chinese government demonstrated a willingness to share fishing resources because of its larger goal of geopolitical importance: limiting the U.S. military presence in the region.

[f]For this positive view, see [43].

[g]When Aquino was president, China essentially took control of the Shoal in 2012 when the Chinese coast guard removed Filipino fishermen from the Shoal in April to June of 2012.

Allowing the Philippines access to the Shoal, in other words, demonstrates how China is acting in a manner to advance itself strategically. With the Chinese government granting the Philippines access to the Shoal, and with Filipino acceptance of that, the Filipino government is working with China on China's terms.[h] Because Duterte, unlike his predecessor, has neither sought to use IOs (such as ASEAN) to gain the upper hand with China nor has he sought to use the international court's ruling in his favor regarding relations with Beijing [30, 49], China views this favorably and thus is willing to work with Duterte, so long as Duterte recognizes China's interests.[i]

4.3.3 *Stage 3: China asserts its control over the sea (mid-March 2017–present)*

In mid-March, China abruptly announced its plans of building a monitoring station for the environment at the Shoal [27]. Shortly after this, Philippine Justice Minister Vitaliano Aguirre stated that the Philippines would seek to improve relations with the U.S. [25]. Duterte issued a statement that he would have military control of the disputed islands. Then, in early April, Duterte deployed the Philippine military to the SCS, in response to China's actions in the area. Duterte even stated his plans of raising the Philippine flag on Pag-asa Island on June 12, the Philippine Independence Day [15]. In addition to Pag-asa Island, Duterte stated that he had ordered the military to display the Philippine flag at additional places, such as islands, reefs, and shoals [28]. In his words: "What's ours now, at least get them and make a strong point there that it is ours." [15].

Based on Duterte's account, Xi Jinping told Duterte to be aware of China's desires. In demonstrating how Xi Jinping wants to make it clear

---

[h] I thank Peter Kreuzer for suggesting this point.

[i] Some may argue that Duterte is seeking to obtain as much as possible for his country, and thus it is not that he is anti-American. In other words, while he has not removed the U.S. military from the Philippines, he has improved ties with China in his quest to obtain even more from the U.S. (I thank Peter Kreuzer for this point). Moreover, some may contend that Duterte does not have clear foreign policy goals, including a lack of a plan for handling SCS issues. This is beyond my focus in this chapter. However, whether or not Duterte is sincere with his anti-American statements, Beijing has welcomed this action, as it means that the U.S. has a tougher time in East Asia in terms of geostrategic interests — and that is what matters for China.

to Duterte that the Philippines must know where it stands, Duterte, in a public announcement on May 19, 2017, stated that Xi told him to be prepared for war with China if Duterte followed through with the international court's decision that dismissed China's position on the SCS [52]. Xi's warning to Duterte regarding China's willingness to go to war with the Philippines was sparked by Duterte's interest in drilling for oil. Xi, in short, wanted to make it clear to Duterte both where China stands on this issue of control over the South China Sea and that in Xi's view of the Philippines does not have possession of the Shoal. With having access to fishing, as mentioned previously, the Philippines is having such access based on China's terms. Fishing under the auspices of Chinese rule is very different from the Philippines drilling for oil on its own. China, in short, wants to be in control of what the Philippines does in the SCS and not have the Philippines take matters into their own hands regarding drilling for oil. On that same day, May 19, 2017, the Chinese government released a joint press statement from China and the Philippines lauding the meeting the two countries had regarding the desire to cooperate on SCS issues [44].

During a meeting between Chinese foreign minister Wang Yi and the Philippines' foreign minister, Alan Cayetano, Wang Yi stated: "China is willing to be the most genuine and lasting cooperation partner on the road of the Philippines' national development and revitalization" [46]. Wang Yi went on to add, "China firmly supports the Philippines in pursuing an independent foreign policy." With the previous statement, Wang Yi meant that China welcomes the break that the Philippines has had with the U.S. China's foreign minister went on to add that the recent improvement in China–Philippines relations has played a central role in improving the situation in the SCS. He added that in the event "certain forces outside of the region" (i.e., the U.S.) seek to disrupt the situation in the SCS, then ASEAN states need to unify and denounce such outside forces.

4.4 Discussion and Implications

4.4.1 *China's quest for power*

When examining why China's relations with the Philippines have changed dramatically from one leader (i.e., Aquino) to the next (i.e., Duterte), we need to consider the larger geopolitical events in the region and the role of the U.S. As argued throughout this chapter, the Chinese government has sought to advance its main objective in this case here, that is, to limit the U.S. in the SCS and advance China's standing in the SCS. Trading fishing access for limiting the U.S. is an obvious choice for the Chinese government. Put differently, the Chinese government is willing to work with Duterte because he is embracing a fundamentally different policy than his predecessor. If other countries in the region are willing to act in a similar manner as Duterte (i.e., chart a foreign policy course that is not in line with the U.S. and instead both embrace China), then chances for an improvement with China appear promising so long as such countries recognize that China is the ultimate decision-maker, as demonstrated in this case.

In addition to the case examined here, there are numerous examples that also demonstrate this pattern of China acting in a way to assert itself militarily in the Asia-Pacific and limit the U.S. military presence in the region, such as constructing artificial islands for the purpose of military force, increase in number of cases in which the Chinese Coast Guard has played an aggressive role in confronting other countries' coast guard or ships in the region [51], and how the Chinese coast guard was involved in the majority of conflicts in the South China Sea from 2010–2016 [31]. Moreover, China's joint naval exercises with Russia in the Pacific near the *Diaoyu/Senkaku* Islands demonstrates that China is willing to side with a leading U.S. adversary in conducting such naval exercises. These examples, which are all related to military issues, especially the creation of islands for military purposes, demonstrate how China is acting in a way that is different from how it acted in the 1980s and 1990s. In the 1990s, China was not the economic and military power that it is today, and such power needs to be considered when examining why China is acting differently.

As a result of acquiring such new power, China has aimed to assert itself by advancing various new initiatives such as the Belt and Road Initiative (BRI) and the Asia Infrastructure Investment Bank (AIIB). It was not possible for China to take such bold steps twenty years ago.[j] All of these new Chinese initiatives are best explained by the view that as states acquire more power, such states assert themselves accordingly in world politics. In this case, we see how China operates strategically to maximize its security.

[j] An in-depth examination of Xi's initiatives is beyond my scope here.

Because Duterte publicly stated that he made the case to Beijing regarding his desire to have Philippine fishermen access to the Shoal, which was then approved Beijing, the implications are significant in terms of perception. Xi could have held on to the view that reversing his actions and moving ahead with such a call from Duterte would result in him being perceived as weak both by his domestic audience and internationally, and thus was a risk he could not take. If the Chinese government were concerned about the potential precedent that this may establish or the signal that this may send to other states in the SCS, then it would not have reversed its decision. Instead, this demonstrates that China is more interested in limiting the U.S. in the region and willing to engage with another state so long as that state is perceived as being willing to work with China on China's terms.

4.4.2 *The role of the U.S.*

Given the U.S. military presence in the Asia Pacific with Japan, South Korea, Singapore, Vietnam and U.S. support for Taiwan, the Chinese government wants to limit such a U.S. security presence in the region and work with partners who will go against such a U.S.-led security system in the region. China has had numerous tensions with Japan in recent years regarding the disputed ownership of the *Diaoyu/Senkaku* Islands. Since the U.S. has a security treaty with Japan, China is cognizant of how any conflict with Japan could involve the U.S., and the same with South Korea. Therefore, given the situation in the Asia Pacific, the case of China–Philippines relations and the evolution needs to be placed in such context.

In terms of policy implications, Glaser's suggestions are relevant here, as he argued that the U.S. should work out a deal (or what Glaser calls a "grand bargain") with China that the U.S. will not defend Taiwan in a confrontation with China [11]. In exchange for the U.S. doing so, China would have to agree to "peacefully resolve its maritime and land disputes in the South China and East China Seas, and officially accept the United States' long-term military security role in East Asia." [2015] According to Glaser, if the U.S. is not aggressive with China and does not engage in actions that are perceived as threatening by China, China will feel more secure and relations will improve between the two countries [10, 11].[k] For Glaser, as argued throughout this chapter, China's actions need to be

[k]For a critical assessment of Glaser on this topic, see [8].

viewed in the larger context of U.S. military presence and U.S. policies in the region. While Taiwan is of utmost importance for China in terms of having the island return to mainland China, the U.S. military presence in Asia Pacific is also a major concern for China. Therefore, regarding the type of deal with China that Glaser advocates, a U.S. security role in Asia does not appear something that Beijing is willing to agree to.

Based on the fundamental shift in Chinese actions with island building and coast guard incidents in the South China Sea in the post-financial crisis world, it is tough to see how China would accept a U.S. security presence in the region, which is what Glaser calls for, if China's economic and military power increases even more in the years to come. Furthermore, given that China's actions internationally have embraced a more assertive role, starting under Hu Jintao and expanding significantly under Xi, such a desire for more power in international politics could certainly continue in that trajectory, which demolishes Glaser's notion of aiming for a grand bargain.

The grand bargain that Glaser focuses on may be able to achieve peace in the short term, but in the long term, based on how China has demonstrated that it wants more power in the region and the world, such a grand bargain does not appear to be viable. A fundamental objective of the Chinese government is to have the U.S. military presence out of the SCS, and that is what China is aiming to do. That was demonstrated when Chinese stationed at such islands told a U.S. Navy reconnaissance plane flying over China's artificially built islands with military installations: "U.S. military aircraft, this is [the] Chinese military. China has sovereignty over the Nansha Islands. Leave immediately and keep off to avoid any misunderstanding." [38]

Throughout his presidency, Trump has not developed strong ties with Duterte, and this has an impact on China–Philippines relations. When American Secretary of State Mike Pompeo visited the Philippines in March 2019, he stated that if the Philippines were attacked, this would result in the U.S. military coming to its defense. Both the Philippine foreign minister and defense minister, however, emphasized that the topic should not be talked about due to the potential negative consequences [50]. The Filipino defense minister expressed his frustration with the U.S.–Philippines Mutual Defense Treaty (MDT), as he is worried that if there were to be a conflict, it could escalate due to that treaty. The defense secretary stated that the Philippines does not want to get involved in a war with China because of something that the U.S. did in the SCS [36].

Reflecting how negative relations between the U.S. and the Philippines have become, the Philippine defense secretary talked publicly about ending the security alliance. Unlike the Aquino administration, the Duterte administration does not want the U.S. to make any noise regarding the SCS and is concerned that the U.S. is doing more harm than good in that respect [50]. The current Philippine government views the U.S. as too fickle, for previous U.S. presidents have not been explicit in their support for the Philippines if the Philippines were to be attacked or if disputed territory were seized. Regarding such inaction on the part of the U.S., the Philippine defense minister lamented how the U.S. did nothing in the 1990s when China captured a reef that was claimed by the Philippines [36]. In short, the Duterte administration does not want to be in the position in which it has to rely on the U.S. for security assistance in a confrontation with China, as the U.S. is not perceived as credible. Because of these issues, and due to how Trump has not developed close ties with Duterte, this gives China leverage in its relations with the Philippines. Recognizing that war with China would be futile, the Duterte administration wants to avoid that. Instead, the Duterte administration wants economic development for the Philippines, and China's approach to that is viewed as a better alternative than working with the U.S.

In June 2019, a Chinese boat struck a Philippine boat in the South China Sea. The stranded twenty-two Filipinos on board were saved by a Vietnamese boat that was passing by. At the time of the collision, it was unknown if the Chinese boat's actions were on order from the Chinese government or simply the actions of the individuals involved. Despite this, Duterte has not taken any action to jeopardize his relationship with China or move closer to the U.S.

4.5 Conclusion

Prior to Duterte becoming president, China's relations with the Philippines were very tense. Shortly after Duterte became president, however, China's relations with the Philippines improved dramatically. While China under both Hu Jintao and Xi Jinping demonstrated that it was not interested in cooperating with an IO, China is willing to work bilaterally with the leader of another country (e.g., Duterte) who demonstrates that he is not interested in having good ties with the U.S. and is instead willing to work with China on China's terms.

With this case, China has demonstrated that it is acting to advance its security preference of limiting the U.S. security presence in the region. Given that China is allowing the Philippines to fish at the Shoal, providing the Philippines with loans and investment, China is willing to do such things in order to advance the more important goal. China's desire to have this alliance with Duterte reflects how this is an alliance of convenience for the Chinese government. The Chinese government knows that if they can get the Philippines on its side, then this would hinder the U.S. military presence in the region, which means having good relations with Duterte could be a huge security victory for China.

References

1. Burgess, S. F. (2016). Rising bipolarity in the South China Sea: The American rebalance to Asia and China's expansion. *Contemporary Security Policy*, *37*(1): 111–143.
2. Buzan, B. & Cox, M. (2013). China and the U.S.: Comparable cases of "Peaceful Rise"? *Chinese Journal of International Politics*, *6*(2): 109–132.
3. Callahan, W. A. (2012). China's Strategic Futures. *Asian Survey*, *52*(4): 617–642.
4. Chan, I. & Li, M. (2015). New Chinese leadership, new policy in the South China Sea dispute? *Journal of Chinese Political Science*, *20*: 35–50.
5. Chang-Liao, N. (2016). China's new foreign policy under Xi Jinping. *Asian Security*, *12*(2): 82–91.
6. Cruz De Castro, R. (2016a). The Philippines discovers its maritime domain: The Aquino administration's shift in strategic focus from internal to maritime security. *Asian Security*, *12*(2): 111–131.
7. Cruz De Castro, R. (2016b). The duterte administration's foreign policy: Unraveling the aquino administration's balancing agenda on an emergent China. *Journal of Current Southeast Asian Affairs*, *3*: 139–159.
8. Easley, L., Kim, P., & Glaser, C. L. (2015). Correspondence: Grand bargain or bad idea? U.S. relations with China and Taiwan. *International Security*, *40*(4), 178–191.
9. Friedberg, A. L. (2015). The sources of Chinese conduct: Explaining Beijing's assertiveness. *The Washington Quarterly*, *37*(4): 133–150.
10. Glaser, C. L. (2013). How oil influences U.S. national security. *International Security*, *38*(2): 112–146.
11. Glaser, C. L. (2015). A U.S.-China grand bargain?: The hard choice between military competition and accommodation. *International Security*, *39*(4): 49–90.

12. Heydarian, R. J. (2017). Tragedy of small power politics: Duterte and the shifting sands of Philippine foreign policy. *Asian Security*, *13*(3): 220–236.
13. Hu, W. (2016). Xi Jinping's "Big Power Diplomacy" and China's Central National Security Commission (CNSC). *Journal of Contemporary China*, *25*(98): 163–177.
14. Hughes, C. (2011). Reclassifying Chinese nationalism: The *geopolitik* turn. *Journal of Contemporary China*, *20*(71): 601–620.
15. Kreuzer, P. (2016). A comparison of Malaysian and Philippine responses to China in the South China Sea. *Chinese Journal of International Politics*, *9*(3): 239–276.
16. Le Miere, C. (2014). The spectre of an Asian arms race. *Survival*, *56*(1): 139–156.
17. Murphy, A. M. (2017). Great power rivalries, domestic politics and Southeast Asian foreign policy: Exploring the Linkages. *Asian Security*, *13*(3): 165–182.
18. Rapp-Hooper, M. (2016). Parting the South China Sea: How to uphold the rule of law. *Foreign Affairs*, September/October: 76–82.
19. Walt, S. M. (1985). Alliance formation and the balance of world power. *International Security*, *9*(4): 3–41.
20. Wolf, R. (2011). Respect and disrespect in international politics: The significance of status recognition. *International Theory*, *3*(1): 105–142.
21. Yahuda, M. (2013). China's new assertiveness in the South China Sea. *Journal of Contemporary China*, *22*(81): 446–459.
22. Yan, X. (2014). From keeping a low profile to striving for achievement. *Chinese Journal of International Politics*, *7*(2): 153–184.
23. Zhao, S. (2013). Foreign policy implications of Chinese nationalism revisited: The strident turn. *Journal of Contemporary China*, *22*(81): 535–553.
24. Waltz, K. (1979). *Theory of International Politics.* Waveland Press.
25. Al Jazerra and News Agencies. (2017). Philippines to China: Stop Scarborough Shoal plan. *Al Jazerra*. https://www.aljazeera.com/news/2017/03/philippines-china-stop-scarborough-shoal-plan-170321132520315.html.
26. Allison, G. (2016). Of Course China, Like All Great Powers Will Ignore an International Legal Verdict. *The Diplomat.* https://thediplomat.com/2016/07/of-course-china-like-all-great-powers-will-ignore-an-international-legal-verdict/.
27. American Interest. (2017). China Ready to Cross Red Line at Scarborough Shoal. *American Interest.* https://www.the-american-interest.com/2017/03/17/china-ready-to-cross-a-red-line-at-scarborough-shoal/.
28. Associated Press. (2017). Philippines to Occupy and Fortify Spratly Islands It Holds. *Washington Post.* https://www.washingtonpost.com/world/asia_

pacific/philippines-to-occupy-and-fortify-spratly-islands-it-claims/2017/04/06/ae76f39e-1aa9-11e7-8598-9a99da559f9e_story.html?utm_term=.81e4cc08bd0c.

29. Brady, A. (2014). Chinese Foreign Policy: A New Era Dawns. *The Diplomat.* https://thediplomat.com/2014/03/chinese-foreign-policy-a-new-era-dawns/.
30. Camroux, D. (2016). *Duterte's undermining of ASEAN.* East Asia Forum. https://www.eastasiaforum.org/2016/11/26/dutertes-undermining-of-asean/.
31. China Power Project. (2020). *Are maritime law enforcement forces destabilizing Asia?* CSIS. https://chinapower.csis.org/maritime-forces-destabilizing-asia/.
32. Cohen, J. A. (2016). *Like it or not, UNCLOS arbitration is legally binding for China.* East Asia Forum. https://www.eastasiaforum.org/2016/07/11/like-it-or-not-unclos-arbitration-is-legally-binding-for-china/.
33. Delizo, M. J. T. (2016). Chinese eyes "wholesale" access for PH at Patang. *The Manila Times.* https://www.manilatimes.net/2016/11/27/news/top-stories/china-eyes-wholesale-access-ph-panatag/298627/.
34. Feng, H. (2016). *Power play in the South China Sea.* East Asia Forum. https://www.eastasiaforum.org/2016/10/06/power-play-in-the-south-china-sea/.
35. Foreign Ministry Affairs. (2015). Foreign Ministry Spokesperson Hua Chunying's Regular Press Conference on May 8, 2015. Retrieved from https://www.fmprc.gov.cn/mfa_eng/xwfw_665399/s2510_665401/2511_665403/t1261981.shtml.
36. Gomez, J. (2019). Philippines worried it may get involved in war at sea for U.S. *AP News.* https://www.apnews.com/c8d36e22d5af478b9fe4bb9b8dd3743b.
37. Kingsbury, D. (2016). *Filipino strongman Duterte not just talk.* East Asia Forum. https://www.eastasiaforum.org/2016/05/24/filipino-strongman-duterte-not-just-talk/?format=pdf.
38. Lendon, B., Watson, I., & Wescott, B. (2018). "Leave immediately": U.S. Navy plane warned over South China Sea. https://www.cnn.com/videos/world/2018/08/10/us-navy-plane-warned-south-china-sea-watson-dnt-vpx.cnn/video/playlists/south-china-sea-dispute/.
39. Lukin, A. (2016). *Will a Russian naval base appear in the South China Sea?* East Asia Forum. https://www.eastasiaforum.org/2016/11/02/will-a-russian-naval-base-appear-in-the-south-china-sea/.
40. Manning, R. A. & Przystup, J. (2016). *What might a new Asian order look like?* East Asia Forum. https://www.eastasiaforum.org/2016/04/12/what-might-a-new-asian-order-look-like/.
41. Masuda, M. (2016). *Why has Chinese foreign policy become more assertive?* East Asia Forum. https://www.eastasiaforum.org/2016/02/20/why-has-chinese-foreign-policy-become-more-assertive/.
42. Ministry of Foreign Affairs. (2016). *Xi Jinping Sends Message to Congratulate Rodrigo Duterte on His Inauguration as President of the Philippines.*

43. Ministry of Foreign Affairs. (2016). *Li Keqiang talks with President Rodrigo Duterte of the Philippines.* http://www.china-embassy.org/eng/zgyw/t1511465.htm.
44. Ministry of Foreign Affairs. (2017). *Joint press release for the first meeting of the China-Philippines Bilateral Consultation Mechanism on the South China Sea.* https://www.fmprc.gov.cn/mfa_eng/wjdt_665385/wshd_665389/t1463538.shtml.
45. Ministry of Foreign Affairs. (2017). *Joint Statement between the government of the People's Republic of China and the government of the Republic of the Philippines.* https://www.fmprc.gov.cn/mfa_eng/wjdt_665385/2649_665393/t1511299.shtml.
46. Ministry of Foreign Affairs. (2017). *Wang Yi: China firmly supports the Philippines in pursing an independent foreign policy.* https://www.fmprc.gov.cn/mfa_eng/zxxx_662805/t1480545.shtml.
47. Moore, Gregory J. (2016). It's Not Just Material: Politics, Culture and Ideas Might Drive China into Confrontation. *The National Interest.* https://nationalinterest.org/feature/china-talks-about-harmony-feeds-global-disorder-17136.
48. Panda, A. (2016). South China Sea: What Exactly has Changed at Scarborough Shoal. *The Diplomat.* https://thediplomat.com/2016/11/south-china-sea-what-exactly-has-changed-at-scarborough-shoal/.
49. Reuters. (2017). China Expresses Concern Over Reported Duterte South China Sea Comments. Online at https://www.usnews.com/news/world/articles/2017-04-07/china-expresses-concern-over-reported-duterte-south-china-sea-comments.
50. Tweed, D. (2018). Military control of Chinese coast guard adds edge to sea disputes. *The Japan Times.* https://www.japantimes.co.jp/news/2018/03/27/asia-pacific/military-control-chinese-coast-guard-adds-edge-sea-disputes/.
51. Villamor, F. (2017). Duterte Orders Military to Parts of South China Sea Claimed by Philippines. *New York Times.* https://www.nytimes.com/2017/04/06/world/asia/rodrigo-duterte-south-china-sea.html.
52. White, H. (2016). *South China Sea: After the Hague ruling, what's next?* East Asia Forum. https://www.eastasiaforum.org/2016/07/07/south-china-sea-after-the-hague-ruling-whats-next/.
53. Zhang, H. (2008). Torchbearer invited to visit France again. *China Daily.* Online at http://www.chinadaily.com.cn/olypmics/2008-04/22/content_6673994.htm.

https://doi.org/10.1142/9781786349286_0005

Chapter 5

U.S. Foreign Policy in the South China Sea

Barry Balleck

5.1 Introduction

The South China Sea is one of the most heavily traveled waterways in the world, contributing to "around one third of world trade" [23]. The waters are particularly critical for China, as well as Brunei, Malaysia, the Philippines, Taiwan, and Vietnam. The United Nations Conference on Trade and Development (UNCTAD) "estimates that roughly 80% of global trade by volume and 70% by value is transported by sea," with 60% of all global trade passing through Asia [23]. As the world's second-largest economy, the South China Sea is critical to China's continued economic success, and unimpaired travel through the waterway is necessary to maintain China's upward economic trajectory. Yet because the South China Sea is such a critical waterway bordered by so many Asian countries dependent upon access to vital sea lanes, freedom of access within the waters has become very hotly contested in recent years. As noted by the U.S. Congressional Research Service:

> China is part to multiple territorial disputes in the South China Sea (SCS) and the East China Sea (ECS), including, in particular, disputes with multiple neighboring countries over the Paracel Islands, Spratly Islands, and Scarborough Shoal in the SCS, and with Japan over the Senkaku Islands in the ECS. Up through 2014, U.S. concern over these

> disputes centered more on their potential for causing tension, incidents, and a risk of conflict between China and its neighbors in the region, including U.S. allies, Japan, and the Philippines and emerging partner states such as Vietnam. While that concern remains, particularly regarding the potential for a conflict between China and Japan involving the Senkaku Islands, U.S. concern since 2014 (i.e., since China's island-building activities in the Spratly Islands were first publicly reported) has shifted increasingly on how China's strengthening position in the SCS may be affecting the risk of a U.S.-China crisis or conflict in the SCS and the broader U.S.-Chinese strategic competition [19].

Recognizing the vital role that the South China Sea plays in its national security, China has constructed numerous military outposts on several artificial islands on "tiny reefs and shoals in the South China Sea" — all built in disputed waters, thus increasing military and economic tensions in the area [9]. As such, China has staked a claim to its hegemony over the region, recognizing that its island-creating activities have heightened tensions in the region, to levels perhaps unseen since World War II. Considering the long-standing territorial disputes of the countries bordering the SCS, China's actions have been met by widespread international condemnation. Since 2015, the United States, the United Kingdom, and France have conducted freedom of navigation operations (FONOP) in the disputed waters of the South China Sea. These actions have the potential in the coming years to bring powerful military forces in conflict with one another as both China and the United States assert themselves within this important waterway. This chapter shall examine the current conflict between the United States and China and speculate as to what the future of the South China Sea might hold for both countries.

5.2 Background

During World War II, the Empire of Japan seized and occupied several islands within the South China Sea, claiming that the islands did not legitimately belong to any single country within the region. To further its war effort, the Imperial Japanese Navy took control of the islands and conducted various military operations from the islands, using them as bases of operation. At the end of World War II, Imperial Japan relinquished control of most of the islands that it had occupied as a result of the 1951 Treaty of San Francisco, the treaty which re-established peaceful relations between Japan and most of the allied powers of World War II. The San Francisco Treaty, however, did not define any territorial rights to the island that Japan had occupied, nor did it specify the status of these islands. At the time, the newly founded People's Republic of China (PRC) made various claims on the islands, as it did again during the 1958 Taiwan Strait Crisis in which the PRC attempted to "liberate" Taiwan from the occupation of the Chinese Nationalist Party, or Kuomintang.

Over the next 50+ years, the PRC would continue to assert its claims over the disputed islands in the South China Sea, as well as put forth its claim of its historical right to maintain a hegemonic claim over the area. After the 2008–2009 U.S. financial crisis, China wrongly assumed that the United States was in "terminal decline," both economically and militarily, and that this was the moment to undo a century of humiliation by asserting its increased influence rather than biding its time as its economy continued to develop [22]. China asserts that "it has a historical claim to virtually the entire [South China] sea. The other countries on the sea's perimeter argue China is violating international treaties, infringing on their fishing and exploration rights, and staking out military positions that could give it the edge in a future conflict" [17]. The map upon which China bases its claim of sovereignty in the South China — formerly an obscure relic of Nationalist rule in the early 20th century — quickly became famous around the world for its most important feature, a loop in the form of nine dashes that droops hundreds of miles from China's southernmost province, the island of Hainan, and approaches the shores of several Southeast Asian nations to enclose one of the world's most important waterways. The map made China's neighbors notice that the region's largest country was turning boldly revisionist as it grew in strength. For the time being, though, some may have been reassured by their belief that most of the world would scorn China's attempt at cartographic fiat as fundamentally baseless [17]. As noted by American journalist Steve Mollman writing in *Quartz*, the "nine-dash line," which initially included 11 lines, was adopted by the Chinese Communist Party in 1949, but later they decided to remove two dashes.

Nevertheless, in 2009, Beijing submitted [the] "nine-dash line" map to the U.N., encompassing 90% of the South China Sea as its maritime claim. UNCLOS (United Nations Convention on the Law of the Sea) and other maritime laws grant greater maritime rights to habitable islands than to rocks and reefs. Therefore, China is trying to create such islands, and, in doing so, claim both 12 nautical miles, or almost 14 miles, of territorial waters around each feature, as well as an exclusive economic zone of 200 nautical miles, or just over 230 miles, around each. Chinese forces occupy features in the Paracel Islands and continue to "reclaim" land through both the Paracels and Spratlys.

Beginning in 2013, China began its construction of artificial islands across wide areas of the South China Sea. To date, China has created over 3,200 acres of land out of what before had just been ocean reefs. This construction of these islands has led to "the loss of thousands of acres of reef in recent years [and] constitutes the quickest rate of permanent loss of coral reefs in human history" [14]. As noted by Professor John McManus, a leading marine biologist, who analyzed satellite photos of the artificial islands being created by the Chinese,

> Coral has been drowned in sand and marine ecosystems have been devastated .... The sand and silt stirred up by the dredgers covers most of the lagoon and is settling out on most of the remaining reef. The sand will kill nearly any bottom-dwelling organisms on which it settles in large quantities and clog the gills of most fish .... Dredged silt can be seen to be forming in strands instead of plumes. This is caused by a reaction from the millions of tiny polyps on the coral reef to the dredging, exuding copious amounts of mucous in a desperate attempt to remove the sediment [14].

5.3 What is China's End Game?

To what end has China undertaken its ambitious and provocative building of artificial land in the South China Sea? As noted by Howard W. French, an author and associate professor at the Columbia School of Journalism,

> There is no single explanation for why asserting its authority over the South China Sea now matters so much to China. Controlling the many tiny islands is in part a matter of controlling of the wealth assumed to lay beneath the sea in the form of unexploited minerals and oil and gas, not to mention the immense fisheries that exist in these waters. It is in part a matter of increasing the country's sense of security, by dominating the maritime approaches to its long coast, and securing sea lanes to the

> open Pacific. It is in part a matter of overcoming historical grievances. And finally, it is about becoming a power at least on par with the U.S.: a goal that Chinese leaders are themselves somewhat coy about, but which is now increasingly entering the public discourse [12].

Today, China, by asserting its claims in the South China Sea, has signaled its intention to the world that it is committed to rivaling American naval power in East Asia. But to do so, China realizes that it must first assert preeminent control over what it considers its own home waters. In order to achieve this goal, China has pushed a theory of international law that runs contrary to the interpretation held by the United States and most other nations. The general consensus of the law, as articulated by the United Nations Convention on the Law of the Sea (UNCLOS), is that every country which borders a maritime body has a 200-nautical-mile margin known as the exclusive economic zone, or EEZ. This EEZ allows coastal states to assume "jurisdiction over the exploration and exploitation of marine resources in its adjacent section of the continental shelf, taken to be a band extending 200 miles from the shore .... Within this area, nations claim and exercise sovereign rights and exclusive fishery management authority overall fish and all Continental Shelf fishery resources," while allowing "innocent passage" of military vessels [18]. However, China along with India and Brazil, hold that "activity by foreign military vessels — including intelligence gathering – is excluded in other nations' EEZs unless they are granted permission" [1]. Thus, by its construction of artificial islands, China is attempting to assert its control of territorial waters into the South China Sea in order to limit the reach of the U.S. Seventh Fleet, which has patrolled the area since the end of World War II.

For their part, China maintains that its claims on the South China Sea and its various islands have been formed "over the long course of history" and have an "adequate historical and legal basis" [13]. China has stated that its construction work is "lawful, reasonable, and justified," and that the construction "does not target or affect anyone" [25]. The Chinese claim that "freedom of navigation" is not at issue in the South China Sea, though they point out that this concept "should not be used as an excuse to infringe upon the sovereignty, rights, and security of coastal countries," a not-so-subtle warning to the United States that it must respect the growing military power of China, and recognize its hegemonic claim to the South China Sea area.

5.4 China's Actions and its Effects on its Neighbors

Soon after China began its island-building policy, the Philippines — along with three other South China Sea members; i.e., Brunei, Malaysia, and Vietnam — filed a case with the Hague's Permanent Court of Arbitration disputing China's right to build the artificial islands as well as claim the maritime resources contained within the "nine-dash line." Another South China Sea neighbor — Indonesia — became increasingly assertive regarding China's actions and began to push back against Beijing's "far-reaching claims." In fact, Indonesia has impounded and sunk more than 50 foreign boats — "including from Vietnam, Malaysia and China" — "to deter illegal fishing in its waters" [11]. Nevertheless, Chinese fishermen, emboldened by China's claims to the South China Sea and protected by Chinese Coast Guard ships, continually encroach upon Indonesian waters. Though the sinking of foreign vessels seems drastic, Indonesian Fisheries Minister Susi Pudjiastuti has stated that "There's no other way," as Indonesia has "suffered great economic loss from lax regulations that gave leeway to foreign boats to fish in Indonesian waters" [11].

For its part, China has "bristled" at Indonesia's determination to protect what it believes are its territorial waters. China has acknowledged that the two countries have overlapping claims in the waters of the South China Sea. Yet China has reasserted its historic rights to all the waters in the South China Sea, whether for fishing or oil and gas drilling.

China's determination to assert what it believes are its "historic rights" in the South China Sea has caused other neighboring countries to push back against Chinese heavy-handedness. In January 2016, the Philippines approved the return of U.S. naval forces to the Subic Bay naval base after a quarter-century absence. In addition, the United States lifted an arms embargo on Vietnam and the once mortal enemies have demonstrated a willingness to cooperate with one another on matters of defense. Indeed, not long after the U.S. lifting of the arms embargo, Vietnam reopened the deep-water harbor of Cam Ranh Bay to U.S. Navy warships. Considered one of the finest deep-water shelters in Southeast Asia, Cam Ranh Bay was significantly upgraded by the United States to serve as a base of operations during the Vietnam War. Allowing the United States back into Vietnamese territory, therefore, allows Vietnam to signal to China its willingness to push back against Chinese intentions in the South China Sea.

Though China has challenged "the customary and treaty law of the sea by claiming 'indisputable sovereignty' across a massive swath of Southeast Asian waters and skies," a U.S. presence in Cam Ranh Bay allows "the United States to uphold freedom of navigation in the 1.4 million-square mile [South China] sea." As pointed out by Carl Thayer, Emeritus Professor at the University of New South Wales,

> There is no operational imperative for the U.S. to acquire a "stop over point" between Singapore and Taiwan. The United States 7th Fleet is home ported in Yokosuka, Japan. The U.S. maintains Naval Base Guam, a major naval facility. Some of the U.S. Navy ships that visit the South China Sea are based in San Diego and Pearl Harbor, Hawaii. U.S. warships are capable of at-sea replenishment.
>
> Vietnam and the United States have held on and off again discussions about raising their Obama era comprehensive partnership to a strategic partnership. In light of China's persistent bullying of Vietnam over sovereignty, maritime disputes and oil exploration in the South China Sea some analysts argue that the "circumstances and specific conditions" may have arisen for a change of policy [24].

In July 2016, the Hague's Permanent Court of Arbitration finally ruled on the Philippines case and declared that "China has no legal basis to claim historic rights to the waters within its so-called 'nine-dash line'" [3]. Moreover, the Court declared that China's "island construction and coast guard activities … violated the Philippines' sovereign rights in its exclusive economic zone" [3]. China, of course, dismissed The Hague Tribunal's ruling stating that by its actions China was not only safeguarding its national sovereignty but also protecting the integrity and legitimacy of the maritime rights of all nations [4]. Indeed, China's strategy was to discredit the Tribunal's credibility by pointing out irregularities with which the decision had been rendered. China argued:

> The unilateral initiation of arbitration by the Philippines is out of bad faith. It aims not to resolve the relevant disputes between China and the Philippines, or to maintain peace and stability in the South China Sea, but to deny China's territorial sovereignty and maritime rights and interests in the South China Sea. The initiation of this arbitration violates international law. First, the subject-matter of the arbitration initiated by the Philippines is in essence an issue of territorial sovereignty over some

> islands and reefs of Nansha Qundao (the Nansha Islands), and inevitably concerns and cannot be separated from maritime delimitation between China and the Philippines. Fully aware that territorial issues are not subject to UNCLOS, and that maritime delimitation disputes have been excluded from the UNCLOS compulsory dispute settlement procedures by China's 2006 declaration, the Philippines deliberately packaged the relevant disputes as mere issues concerning the interpretation or application of UNCLOS. Second, the Philippines' unilateral initiation of arbitration infringes upon China's right as a state party to UNCLOS to choose on its own will the procedures and means for dispute settlement. As early as in 2006, pursuant to Article 298 of UNCLOS, China excluded from the compulsory dispute settlement procedures of UNCLOS disputes concerning, among others, maritime delimitation, historic bays or titles, military and law enforcement activities. Third, the Philippines' unilateral initiation of arbitration violates the bilateral agreement reached between China and the Philippines, and repeatedly reaffirmed over the years, to resolve relevant disputes in the South China Sea through negotiations. Fourth, the Philippines' unilateral initiation of arbitration violates the commitment made by China and ASEAN Member States, including the Philippines, in the 2002 Declaration on the Conduct of Parties in the South China Sea (DOC) to resolve the relevant disputes through negotiations by states directly concerned. By unilaterally initiating the arbitration, the Philippines violates UNCLOS and its provisions on the application of dispute settlement procedures, the principle of "pacta sunt servanda" and other rules and principles of international law [16].

As noted by Fu Ying, a former Chinese Vice Minister of Foreign Affairs and Ambassador to the United Kingdom, "There is no such thing as absolute power in international law." A commentary from a Chinese newspaper soon after The Hague ruling reiterated the Chinese disdain for the validity of the proceedings as the editor noted:

> The U.S. actions near China, particularly those on the South China Sea Issues, are part of its [the U.S.] Asia-Pacific Rebalance strategies. Its intentions are no more than containing China to preserve its interests in the Asia Pacific region and its global hegemony. The U.S. motives are apparent to the world, especially to the Chinese people. The current China is nothing like the country it was one hundred years ago. Any act that tries to violate China's territorial sovereignty will fail [26].

The Chinese Foreign Ministry official statement regarding The Hague ruling went on to reassert China's historical claims while couching China's argument in terms of territorial sovereignty and maritime rights:

> China's territorial sovereignty and maritime rights and interests in the South China Sea shall under no circumstances be affected by those awards. China opposes and will never accept any claim or action based on those awards. The Chinese government reiterates that, regarding territorial issues and maritime delimitation disputes, China does not accept any means of third-party dispute settlement or any solution imposed on China. The Chinese government will continue to abide by international law and basic norms governing international relations as enshrined in the *Charter of the United Nations*, including the principles of respecting state sovereignty and territorial integrity and peaceful settlement of disputes, and continue to work with states directly concerned to resolve the relevant disputes in the South China Sea through negotiations and consultations on the basis of respecting historical facts and in accordance with international law, so as to maintain peace and stability in the South China Sea [16].

5.5 U.S. Policy Toward China in the South China Sea

China's refusal to submit to The Hague Tribunal's ruling in July 2016 exposes the greatest flaw of international law; i.e., that such law is created with the agreement and the acquiescence of state parties, but if those same state parties refuse to abide by the principles of said law, there is little or no recourse for aggrieved parties. In other words, with no supranational authority in the international system to enforce rulings, there is very little that a country such as the Philippines — or Brunei, or Indonesia, or Malaysia, or Vietnam — can do to dissuade a behemoth such as China.

After the election of each new U.S. president in the 21st century, Beijing has precipitated a crisis with Washington in order to test the U.S. resolve. In March 2001, a mere two months after his inauguration, President George W. Bush faced a crisis in the South China Sea when a Chinese frigate rammed the USNS *Bowditch*, followed by a spy plane collision some weeks later. Then, in March 2009, again just a few weeks after his inauguration, President Barack Obama was confronted by the USNS *Impeccable* incident in which five Chinese vessels surrounded the ship 75 miles south of Hainan Island and harassed it in an attempt to provoke an incident [13].

Before Donald Trump was took office, however, the Chinese seized a U.S. underwater drone associated with the USNS *Bowditch.* Like the USNS *Impeccable*, the ship is an unarmed vessel with a predominantly civilian crew whose mission is surveillance and ocean research. Though the U.S. claims the activities of such vessels to be within its rights under the terms of the UN Convention on the Law of the Sea (UNCLOS), China's reasoning is that

> … freedom of navigation and over flight in the EEZ should not include the freedom to conduct military and reconnaissance activities, to perform military deterrence or battlefield preparation, or intelligence gathering. China maintains these activities infringe on the coastal state's national security interests and can be considered a use of force, or a threat to use force, against the state, particularly with the advanced technologies used by the vessels [8].

Whereas the 2001 *Bowditch* took place in the Yellow Sea, "within a couple of hundred miles of the Chinese coast," and the *Impeccable* incident was some 75 miles off of China's coast, the seizure of the underwater drone was some 600 miles from China. The incident did not appear to signal a significant shift in Chinese policy in the South China Sea by though the incident did occur in an area just 57 nautical miles northwest of Subic Bay in the Philippines — an area well within the Philippines exclusive EEC. Rather it was more likely in response to then-President-elect Trump's phone call on December 2, 2016 in which President-elect Trump indicated to Taiwanese President Tsai ing-wen America's willingness to reconsider its "One-China" policy. Trump added additional motivation for the Chinese to react when he made comments to *Fox News* a little more than a week later that "the United States was under no obligation to follow the One-China policy." [7]

Why does the United States continue to patrol the waters of the South China Sea, some 6,000 miles from Hawaii and nearly 9,000 miles from the U.S. mainland? As American author and journalist Howard W. French notes, the first reason is to demonstrate how great powers should interpret and maintain maritime law. It is the avowed policy of the United States to support and uphold international law when it deems such a policy to be in its best interest. In the case of the South China Sea, a U.S. naval presence in the area protects the vital waterway and maintains the commitment that the U.S. has made to neighboring countries, particularly Japan, since the end of World War II. Were the United States to grant China a free hand in the South China Sea, its unopposed control of this vital waterway could embolden the Chinese to make other territorial assertions, particularly in regard to Taiwan. China could also exert enormous economic control by threatening military actions against traversing shipping taking place in waters in its control. The second reason, and perhaps the most important of all, for a continued U.S. naval presence in the South China is a purely strategic one:

> China possesses a much smaller nuclear arsenal than the United States. Survivability for any credible Chinese second-strike capability depends heavily on nuclear-armed submarines that operate from Hainan. The United States patrols the waters of the South China Sea with the world's most advanced anti-submarine monitoring and warfare capabilities, and — to China's great irritation — the Pentagon constantly monitors submarine traffic from Hainan to collect acoustic and operational intelligence [17].

America's decision to "invest its might and prestige in such a faraway dispute" is that, for now, "the United States is the only country that has both the means and the self-assurance to do so. China's rival claimants, countries like the Philippines and even Vietnam, know that to confront Beijing so directly would invite defeat or humiliation. And this is exactly why proponents of American action regard it as imperative [17].

In June 2017, then-U.S. Secretary of State James Mattis further articulated U.S. policy in the South China Sea area. He noted that U.S. Vice President Mike Pence, who had visited the region a few weeks earlier, had reiterated the enduring U.S. commitment to the security and prosperity of the region. This enduring commitment, Mattis said in paraphrasing Pence,

> is based on strategic interests, and on shared values of free people, free markets, and a strong and vibrant economic partnership, a partnership open to all nations, regardless of their size, their populations, or the number of ships in their navies, or any other qualifier. Large nations … large nations, small nations and even shrimps can all thrive in a rules-based order [15].

In his remarks, Secretary of State Mattis proceeded to draw a distinction between the United States and China in both countries' interpretation of international law and the international order:

> I note up front that in the security arena we have a deep and abiding commitment to reinforcing the rules-based international order. This order, as we all know, is a product. It's a true product of so many nations' efforts to create stability. And these efforts, we must remind ourselves, so we don't take them for granted, these efforts grew out of lessons learned the hard way from an economic depression and catastrophic wars.
>
> The international order was not imposed on other nations. Rather, the order is based on principles that were embraced by nations trying to create a better world and restore hope to all.
>
> Those principles have stood the test of time, like equal respect for the international law, regardless of a nation's size or wealth, and freedom of navigation and overflight, including keeping shipping lanes open for all nations' commercial benefit. These principles underwrite stability and build trust, security and prosperity.
>
> The growing prosperity of the people in this region gives proof to the value of institutions, such as the United Nations, ASEAN, the World Bank, the International Monetary Fund, all of which can spur economic growth. They also remind us that each of us have a vested interest in each other's security.
>
> The United States will continue to adapt and continue to expand its ability to work with others to secure a peaceful, prosperous, and free Asia, one with respect for all nations upholding international law. Because we recognize no nation is an island isolated from the others, we stand with our allies and the international community to address pressing security challenges and do so together [15].

Secretary Mattis then turned to China's refusal to recognize the Permanent Court of Arbitration's ruling against Chinese activity in the South China Sea:

> The 2016 ruling by the Permanent Court of Arbitration on the case brought by the Philippines on the South China Sea is binding. We call on all claimants to use this as a starting point to peacefully manage their disputes in the South China Sea. Artificial island construction and

> indisputable militarization of facilities on features in international waters undermine regional stability.
>
> The scope and effect of China's construction activities in the South China Sea differ from those in other countries in several key ways. This includes the nature of its militarization, China's disregard for international law, its contempt for other nations' interests, and its efforts to dismiss non-adversarial resolution of issues.
>
> We oppose countries militarizing artificial islands and enforcing excessive maritime claims unsupported by international law. We cannot and will not accept unilateral coercive changes to the status quo.
>
> *We will continue to fly, sail and operate wherever international law allows, and demonstrate resolve through operational presence in the South China Sea and beyond. Our operations throughout the region are an expression of our willingness to defend both our interests and the freedoms enshrined in international law* [emphasis added] [15].

In his remarks at the Shangri-La Dialogue, Secretary of State Mattis noted that North Korea presents a "clear and present danger" to U.S. national security interests. Yet Jamie Fly, a senior fellow at the German Marshall Fund and previously Senator Marco Rubio's foreign policy advisor, notes that "North Korea is a minor nuisance to U.S. national security compared with the more pressing challenge of China's rise" [10]. Daniel Blumenthal, director of Asian Studies at the American Enterprise Institute, notes that the Obama Administration's "pivot to Asia" policy was not entirely successful, and, in fact, frustrated critical allies, such as Japan, which have been frustrated with U.S. inaction to curb Chinese intentions in the South China Sea. Blumenthal noted that "it is better to take a serious and hardline approach early in a potential conflict of interests, to avoid having to be reactive and escalatory later" [2]. Blumental further noted that a challenger, such as China, will eventually "push too hard," hitting what Blumenthal called, the "U.S. red line." In this case, this leaves the "U.S. with fewer options than it might have had when China was beginning its aggressive push into the South China Sea" [2]. Japan has similarly been frustrated with the U.S. policy of "strategic patience" toward North Korea despite that country's continued pursuit of its nuclear weapons capabilities. The United States must chart a course in the future to enlist its allies in the area to support efforts in confronting China's heavy-handedness in regard to its aggressive actions in the South China Sea.

5.6 Conclusion

Given China's determination to assert what it considers its "historic rights" in the South China, and the United States' equally dogged determination to confront China in this critical area of the world, how can the United States confront the growing challenge of a "rejuvenated" China? Blumenthal believes that the United States must create an Indo-Pacific grand strategy, in line with what Japanese Prime Minister Shinzo Abe has been articulating for years. According to Blumenthal, "building out our new partnerships with Vietnam, Indonesia, and India while strengthening our alliances and partnerships with Japan, Australia, Taiwan, and Singapore will create the maritime encirclement that China most fears" [6]. Blumenthal also asserts that the shrinkage of the U.S. military budget has been problematic for U.S.–China relations. Whereas post-Cold War cuts saw the U.S. Navy with a fleet of more than 400 ships, today the U.S. "struggles to maintain a fleet of 272 deployable battle force ships." [5]. The only manner in which to reassure nervous allies in the South China Sea region who are concerned about the rise of China's power in the South China Sea is to "spend adequate resources on defense" [5].

There are those who are concerned that the Trump Administration views "the Taiwan question" as having "taken on unexpected urgency amid the efforts to secure China's help in reaching a landmark denuclearization agreement with North Korea, as well as ongoing and highly sensitive trade negotiations" [20]. But Jamie Fly asserts that the U.S. must pursue a five-fold strategy in regard to China. First, President Trump must tone down his praise of Chinese leader Xi Jinping. Trump's praise of Xi "muddles the message with allies and partners who are looking for more U.S. leadership in the face of an increasingly aggressive Beijing." Second, the U.S. must continue freedom of navigation operations in the South China Sea, "but also outline publicly why China's actions in these areas are a threat to the global flow of trade and to U.S. interests." Third, advocate for human rights in China. According to Fly, "America's freedom and embrace of universal values is one of the greatest weapons in the struggle against the Communist Party of China and its repressive policies at home and abroad." This strategy appears particularly relevant today in light of the continued protests in Hong Kong aimed at a more responsive and democratic Hong Kong government. Fourth, "develop and begin to implement a regional economic plan" to replace Trump's abandonment of the Trans-Pacific Partnership (TPP). "This needs to change quickly," according to Fly, "as all the military spending in the world will not help if China wins the economic long game." And finally, "the United States needs a China policy that is not single-mindedly focused on issues like North Korea, or even economic disputes. Our China policy must address the long-term strategic challenge posed by China's growing military and economic power" [21].

The United States should understand Chinese intentions. After all, the United States was once an aspiring global power as China is today. But like other aspiring powers of the past that has been checked by their economic, political, and geographical constraints, the only proven method by which China's global ambitions will be muted will be by the concerted efforts of countries determined to confront the challenges that China poses. As the United States still enjoys a position of preeminence in the world, the leader of this concerted effort must be the United States. But it must also be willing to engage its Asian partners as equals in the quest to redefine the strategic relationships that surround the geopolitical issues concerning the South China Sea.

References

1. Geng, J. (2012). The legality of foreign military activities in the exclusive economic zone under UNCLOS. *Merkurious*, *28*(74), pp. 22–30. DOI: http://doi.org/10.5334/ujiel.ax.
2. AEI. (2015). Chinese aggression in the South China Sea. *American Enterprise Institute.* https://www.aei.org/press/chinese-aggression-in-the-south-china-sea/.
3. Beech, H. (2016). Just Where Exactly Did China Get the South China Sea Nine-Dash Line From? *Time.* https://time.com/4412191/nine-dash-line-9-south-china-sea/.
4. Beng, K. K. (2016). China President Xi Dismisses Hague Arbitration on South China Sea by Says "Committed to Peace." *The Straits Times.* https://www.straitstimes.com/asia/east-asia/china-dismisses-hague-ruling-maintains-sovereignty-over-south-china-sea.
5. Blumenthal, D. (2017). China Seeks to Surpass U.S. Influence in Asia. *RealClearWorld.* https://www.realclearworld.com/articles/2017/04/26/china_seeks_to_surpass_us_influence_in_asia_112314.html.
6. Blumenthal, D. (2018). *China's Worldwide Military Expansion.* U.S. House of Representatives. https://docs.house.gov/meetings/IG/IG00/20180517/108298/HHRG-115-IG00-Wstate-BlumenthalD-20180517.pdf.

7. Bohan, C. & Brunnstrom, D. (2016). Trump Says U.S. Not Necessarily Bound by "One China" Policy. *Reuters*. https://www.reuters.com/article/us-usa-trump-china/trump-says-u-s-not-necessarily-bound-by-one-china-policy-idUSKBN1400TY.
8. China-U.S. Focus Staff. (2011). China and U.S. Views on Military Vessel Rights in the EEZ is More than a Legal Matter? *China-US Focus*. https://www.chinausfocus.com/peace-security/china-and-us-views-on-military-vessel-rights-in-the-eez-is-more-than-a-legal-matter.
9. Cloud, D. S. (2015). China's Man-Made Islands in Disputed Waters Raise Worries. *Los Angeles Times*. https://www.latimes.com/world/asia/la-fg-china-us-islands-20150128-story.html.
10. Fly, J. (2018). Dictator Diplomacy. *Washington Examiner*. https://www.washingtonexaminer.com/weekly-standard/dictator-diplomacy.
11. France24 Staff. (2019). Indonesia to Sink Scores of Boats to Deter Illegal Fishing. *France24*. https://www.france24.com/en/20190504-indonesia-sink-scores-boats-deter-illegal-fishing.
12. French, H. W. (2015). What's Behind Beijing's Drive to Control the South China Sea? *The Guardian*. https://www.theguardian.com/world/2015/jul/28/whats-behind-beijings-drive-control-south-china-sea-hainan.
13. Green, M., Hicks, K., Cooper, Z., Schaus, J., & Douglas, J. (2017). Counter-Coercion Series: Harassment of the USN Impeccable. *Asia Maritime Transparency Initiative*. https://amti.csis.org/counter-co-harassment-usns-impeccable/.
14. Holmes, O. (2015). South China Sea Images reveal impact on coral of Beijing's military bases. *The Guardian*. https://www.theguardian.com/world/ng-interactive/2015/sep/17/south-china-sea-images-reveal-impact-on-coral-of-beijings-military-bases.
15. Mattis, J. N. (2017). *The United States and Asia-Pacific security* [Address]. 16th Asia Security Summit The IISS Shangri-La Dialogue, Singapore. https://www.defense.gov/Newsroom/Transcripts/Transcript/Article/1201780/remarks-by-secretary-mattis-at-shangri-la-dialogue/.
16. Ministry of Foreign Affairs. (2016). Statement of the Ministry of Foreign Affairs of the People's Republic of China on the Award of 12 July 2016 of the Arbitral Tribunal in the South China Sea Arbitration Established at the Request of the Republic of the Philippines. https://www.fmprc.gov.cn/mfa_eng/zxxx_662805/t1379492.shtml.
17. Mollman, S. (2016). The Line on a 70-Year-Old Map That Threatens to Set Off a War in East Asia. *Quartz*. https://qz.com/705223/where-exactly-did-chinas-nine-dash-line-in-the-south-china-sea-come-from/.
18. Organization for Economic Cooperation and Development. (2001). Exclusive Economic Zone (EEZ). *OECD*. https://stats.oecd.org/glossary/detail.asp?ID=884.

19. O'Rourke, R. (2020). *U.S.-China strategic competition in South and East China Seas: Background and issues for Congress.* Congressional Research Service. https://crsreports.congress.gov/product/details?prodcode=R42784.
20. Restuccia, A. (2018). "Taiwan Event Creates Headaches for Trump and North Korea Talks. *Politico.* https://www.politico.com/story/2018/05/31/trump-taiwan-north-korea-615253.
21. Rosenberger, L. & Fly, J. (2019). ASD's Laura Rosenberger and Jamie Fly on the Strategerist Podcast. *Alliance for Securing Democracy.* https://securingdemocracy.gmfus.org/asds-laura-rosenberger-and-jamie-fly-on-the-strategerist-podcast/.
22. Schiavenza, M. (2013). How Humiliation Drove Modern Chinese History. *The Atlantic.* https://www.theatlantic.com/china/archive/2013/10/how-humiliation-drove-modern-chinese-history/280878/.
23. Taufan, M. (2019). Traversing the South China Sea: Safety First. *The Diplomat.* https://thediplomat.com/2019/01/traversing-the-south-china-sea-safety-first/.
24. Thayer, C. (2020). Will Vietnam Lease Cam Ranh Bay to the United States? *The Diplomat.* https://thediplomat.com/2020/05/will-vietnam-lease-cam-ranh-bay-to-the-united-states/.
25. The Economic Times. (2015). China Defends South China Sea Projects as Lawful. *The Economic Times.* https://economictimes.indiatimes.com/news/international/business/china-defends-south-china-sea-projects-as-lawful/articleshow/46492769.cms.
26. Xiaohui, W. (2016). S. China Sea Arbitration: A US-led Conspiracy Behind the Farce. *China.org.cn.* http://en.people.cn/n3/2016/0712/c90000-9085051.html.

https://doi.org/10.1142/9781786349286_0006

Chapter 6

One Belt One Road: A Bargain in the South China Sea Disputes

Nalanda Roy

6.1 Introduction

Asia is the world's largest and most populous continent. Asia's rich cultural heritage and history have modernized along with its developing economies, and it is fast becoming one of the world's most dynamic economic regions. Currently, Asia is in the midst of a geopolitical transformation, with vital developments taking place all across the continent. For example, the rise of China and India, the power game between countries to increase commercial influence throughout Eurasia and beyond, and the continued presence of the United States to address this power dynamic are all signs that show that Asia is fast becoming a "flashpoint" on the global platform [8]. Asia is also expected to be the world's largest regional market for natural gas in the next few years. Unprecedented growth is the characteristic of the Asia-Pacific region today, with China at the forefront of rapid economic expansion, followed by India. The 2011 Pacific Energy Summit held in Jakarta, Indonesia, featured the theme "Unlocking the Potential of Natural Gas in the Asia-Pacific." The summit explored the role of natural gas with regard to energy security and climate change in the region [7]. Experts predicted that a Golden Age of gas in the Asia-Pacific region is on its way. In fact, unconventional gas production technology is providing access to vast new reserves of natural gas. At the same time, emerging liquefied natural gas (LNG) infrastructure in the region, rising production, and increased global availability have enabled natural gas to play a significant role in energy diversification efforts.

The International Energy Agency (IEA) projected that China will account for half of the global oil demand growth in the next five years, while over the next 25 years, demand from OECD countries such as the U.S., Japan, and Europe will remain flat [25]. In fact, by 2050, China will consume nearly more than three times the amount of gas it used to consume in 2018. Despite various constraints, new regional pipeline developments have begun to take shape as the continental markets of Asia evolve. Beijing is also enhancing its pipeline diplomacy initiatives to sponsor new major regional gas pipelines from Turkmenistan, Kazakhstan, and Myanmar. The objective is to construct a large west-to-east domestic trunk-line gas pipeline infrastructure to accommodate China's growing imports of LNG [19]. Huge advances in drilling technology and the growing interest of foreign companies in exploring petroleum resources in this region have intensified disputes. Rich hydrocarbon deposits in Brunei and the Malaysian state of Sabah have also been discovered [27].

It is obvious that the SCS dispute has a geostrategic dimension. The SCS has acquired added significance since it harbors large energy reserves. Each state in the region has developed seemingly irreconcilable positions regarding islands and archipelagos. Thus, it often becomes impossible to follow the "good fences make good neighbors" attitudes. The potential riches of the SCS and its adjacent waters have increased competition and conflicts, and thus it might be said that the Asian theater will be critical for shaping state practice regarding the law of the sea and determining whether or not the 1982 convention will be able to resolve matters peacefully. [2] It is estimated that the SCS region, excluding the Paracels and Spratlys, has proven oil reserves of approximately 7.8 billion barrels, and current oil production within the region is well over 1.9 million barrels per day [31]. In fact, total SCS production continues to grow as more and more oil wells in China, Malaysia, and Vietnam have become operational. Some of the world's most important sea lanes, roughly two-thirds of the world's oil, and a third of the world's bulk cargo go through the Strait of Malacca [12], thereby making this region a significant player in the global geostrategic orbit. If China ever succeeds in realizing its territorial claims, it would then "extend its jurisdiction some one thousand nautical miles from its mainland so as to command the virtual Mediterranean or maritime heart of Southeast Asia with far-reaching consequences for the strategic environment." [14]

In 2013, Chinese President Xi Jinping proposed "guojia fuxing" or "national rejuvenation." The idea was the joint construction of the Silk Road Economic Belt and the 21st-Century Maritime Silk Road to reconnect the world, promote world peace, and offer a new direction to the global economy. With the announcement of the opening up of the "New Silk Road" or the Belt and Road Initiative (BRI) or the One Belt One Road (OBOR), both the geoeconomic and the geostrategic scenario in the Asian arena gained new momentum. In keeping with the above background, this chapter critically examines the OBOR strategy (with special reference to the China–Pakistan Economic Corridor) and analyzes whether it can act as a bargain, and even a "soft" balancing strategy in the SCS and be a "game-changer" both in the regional sphere and on the global stage. The chapter discusses whether the Belt and Road Initiative can significantly alter Asia's emerging international order, and even accelerate contests and forge cooperation in the region. This chapter also briefly examines the China–Pakistan Economic Corridor as a case study and explores whether Beijing's assertive policies in the South China Sea and OBOR are contradictory. Finally, the chapter concludes with a brief summary of the results of the bargain and its possible implications in Asian geopolitics.

6.2 OBOR — An Initiative or a Bargain?

More than 2,000 years ago, the Chinese Emperor Zhang Qian helped establish the Silk Road that later formed the foundation for development and prosperity in the entire region [18]. This network of trade routes linked China to Central Asia, the Arab world, and beyond, via one of China's most important exports — silk. President Xi said "... in promoting this initiative, China will follow the principle of wide consultation, joint contribution, and shared benefits [16]. The development programs will be open and inclusive, not exclusive. They will be a real chorus comprising all countries along the routes, not a solo for China itself. To develop the Belt and Road is not to replace existing mechanisms or initiatives for regional cooperation. Much to the contrary, we will build on the existing base to help countries align their development strategies and form complementarity." [5] President Xi also organized the first Peripheral Diplomacy Work Conference, and the Central Conference on Work Relating to Foreign Affairs and expressed China's strategic objectives, basic guidelines, and an overall framework for the country's foreign relations [5].

At the China–ASEAN Expo in 2013, Chinese Premier Li Keqiang emphasized the need to build the Maritime Silk Road with an ASEAN orientation to help promote the economic prosperity of the Belt and Road Initiative (BRI) countries. The One Belt One Road (OBOR) plan was based around two core conduits: The Silk Road Economic Belt and the 21st Century Maritime Silk Road. The Belt and Road Initiative (BRI) is an ambitious effort to improve regional cooperation and connectivity on a transcontinental scale. The goal is to connect Asia, Europe, and Africa along five routes. This is a flagship project that aims to transform the economic environment in the region and also enhance regional cooperation. The 21st Century Maritime Silk Road focuses on using Chinese coastal ports to (4) link China with Europe through the South China Sea and the Indian Ocean, and (5) connect China with the South Pacific Ocean through the South China Sea [4]. This demonstrates that the goal of the Maritime Silk Road is to strengthen infrastructure, trade, and investment ties between China and some 65 other countries that account collectively for over 30% of global GDP, 62% of the population, and 75% of known energy reserves.

In December 2014, China proposed the $40 billion (USD) Silk Road Fund that would finance the Belt and Road Initiative. It was decided that the Fund would comply with international market rules and finance, and would solicit active participation from investors like the China–Africa Development Fund and the Asian Infrastructure Investment Bank. On 14 May 2017, President Xi Jinping at the opening ceremony of the "Belt and Road Forum for International Cooperation" announced that China would contribute an additional 100 billion yuan to the Silk Road Fund. According to the Chinese Academy of International Trade and Economic Cooperation (MOFCO), the objective of the One Belt One Road initiative is to realize the "China Dream," which was the slogan advocated by Xi Jinping [32]. Beijing also predicted that China's annual trade with BRI countries will surpass $2.5 trillion by 2025 [28], growing more rapidly than its trade with the rest of the world. Even smaller economies like Pakistan and Bangladesh will receive a big boost. The BRI is supposed to take advantage of international transport routes, core cities, and key ports to further strengthen collaboration and build six international economic cooperation corridors. These have been identified as the New Eurasia Land Bridge, China–Mongolia–Russia, China–Central Asia–West Asia, China–Indochina Peninsula, China–Pakistan, and Bangladesh–China–India–Myanmar links. At times, these projects appear to be mostly aspirational. Besides, China has too much going on with its involvement in the Arctic, cyberspace, and even outer space. The global recession due to the COVID-19 (Corona Virus Disease-19) pandemic has created another hole in the digital Silk Road. Hence, we need to wait and see whether transparency, higher standards of economic sustainability, and environmental protection will be sufficient enough to fulfill China's loftier ambitions to become a global champion.

6.2.1 *Exploring the CPEC axis*

Over the past couple of years, BRI-linked corridor projects — like the China–Pakistan Economic Corridor (CPEC) in Pakistan — have emerged as a major source of tension in Asian geopolitics. The concept of the China–Pakistan Economic Corridor was first discussed by Premier Li Keqiang during his visit to Pakistan in May 2013. At the time, the objective was to build an economic corridor running from Kashgar, Xinjiang, in the north to Pakistan's Gwadar Port in the south [17]. At present, the two governments have mapped out a provisional long-term plan for building highways, railways, oil and natural gas pipelines, and optic fiber networks stretching from Kashgar to Gwadar Port. The significance of both the Karachi and Gwadar port facilities cannot be underestimated. They not only serve as major transshipment points for China's energy and resource needs but also give China direct access to the Persian Gulf and the Horn of Africa — including its naval base in Djibouti — via the Arabian Sea and the Indian Ocean [13].

According to a joint declaration issued by China and Pakistan in Islamabad in April 2015, the two countries have decided to proactively advance key cooperation projects, including Phase II of the upgrade and renovation of the Karakoram Highway (the Thakot–Havelian section), an expressway at the east bay of Gwadar Port, a new international airport, an expressway from Karachi to Lahore (the Multan–Sukkur section), the Lahore rail transport orange line, the Haier-Ruba economic zone, and the China–Pakistan cross-national optic fiber network [20]. There might be a possibility that CPEC could have a useful "demonstration effect, indicating to other investors that Pakistan is a safe and attractive destination for foreign direct investment." [26] A Long-Term Plan for CPEC (2017–2030) was also released in December 2017. The report defines the project broadly as "a growth axis and a development belt," with "the comprehensive transportation corridor and industrial cooperation between

Pakistan and China as the main axis" and "concrete economic and trade cooperation" as "the engine." [21] The CPEC timeline stated that the short-term projects would be completed by the end of 2020, medium-term projects should be close to completion by 2025, and long-term projects should be in place by 2030. As China integrates more with the global economy, it was suspected that Beijing would further open its economy and strengthen its mutually beneficial cooperation with countries in Asia, Europe, and Africa. Although China is broadening global trade and investment links, it is unclear to what extent its growth has been commensurate with provision of global public goods other than perhaps UN peacekeeping assistance and a few other areas. Debate remains about whether China is committed to shouldering more duties and obligations or just appears as a free-rider on global public goods.

The deal granted the Chinese 40 years of operation rights to the port, which is hugely significant for Beijing because it will allow Beijing to save billions in transportation costs, as well as time, and most importantly, give access to the port of Gwadar, which will play a critical role in China's joint plans for a Silk Road Economic Belt and a Maritime Silk Road linking China to Europe and beyond. The China–Pakistan energy corridor would be an expensive proposition for Beijing given the long distances, rugged terrain, transnational threats (Gwadar's Balochistan province is prone to separatist violence), and insurgency movements involved. However, at the geopolitical level, the proposal is attractive because of Gwadar's proximity to the Persian Gulf. All maritime chokepoints, save for the Strait of Hormuz, would be effectively bypassed. Besides, Pakistan is a close ally of China. Therefore, the Chinese leadership seems to be taking the proposal seriously. During President Pervez Musharraf's visit to China in February 2006, the two sides even agreed to upgrade the Karakoram Highway.

Plans for the CPEC were formalized in 2015 when Pakistan and China signed fifty-one agreements and memoranda of understanding on the $46 billion Chinese investment. Pakistan has the potential to serve as a nexus for the Silk Road Economic Belt and the Maritime Silk Road. Over time, an overland link across Pakistan to the Arabian Sea would help alleviate China's heavy dependence on the Malacca and Lombok/ Makassar straits in Southeast Asia. This is a serious concern for China because the Malacca Strait is a very narrow and congested waterway, but the strait is considered vital because it is the shortest route between the Indian and Pacific oceans. More than 60,000 vessels transit the strait each year, carrying 25% of global trade. In fact, 85% of China's oil imports travel through the single chokepoint of the Strait of Malacca [23]. It also meets 50% of its oil demands through imports from the Middle East. Hence, the strait has both geopolitical and geostrategic significance for China, and the leaders have given considerable attention to the "Malacca dilemma." [9] The massive investment package between China and Pakistan will not only pull Pakistan into a geostrategic orbit but will also be a "game-changer" for the region. This deal is essentially a package of major projects that fall into two domains: transportation and energy. The former involves a rail link connecting Gwadar, a deep-sea commercial port on Pakistan's southern coast, to the western Chinese city of Kashgar (an oasis city in China's Xinjiang region); building a 125-mile tunnel linking the two countries; and upgrading a number of existing highways (including the critical Karachi–Lahore section), etc. While the latter concerns building pipelines to transport oil and gas to Kashgar, the completion of the Iran–Pakistan gas pipeline and the creation of various coal, wind, solar, and hydroenergy plants that would add some 10,000 megawatts to energy-starved Pakistan by 2019.

6.2.2 *Gwadar — A critical chokepoint*

The Gwadar Port in Balochistan province has become a major point of contention between China and India. Gwadar is a warm-water, deep-sea port, which is located 400 km away from the Straits of Hormuz. This port has become a critical choke point in the Persian Gulf. The Port is also located on the shores of the Arabian Sea about 533 km from Karachi and 120 km from the Iranian border. Also, 80% of China's imports pass through the Straits of Malacca. Hence, whenever tensions flare up, both of these straits become extremely vulnerable. The Gwadar port development project commenced in 2002 with huge investments by both Chinese and Pakistani investors. The main idea was to transform Gwadar into a dominant port that would benefit the locals. In fact, with the CPEC project and Gwadar, China will be at the doorstep of the Hormuz. China realized that such an arrangement could eventually eliminate the Malacca dilemma. Additionally, it is also the main feature of the China–Pakistan Economic Corridor, and the key to the Belt and Road initiative because the port is at the heart of the $50 billion Chinese investment in the CPEC. Hence, it is essential for Beijing to develop Gwadar, so that they would have a firm and reliable long-term beachhead in not only the Indian Ocean but also the Persian Gulf, thereby effectively making China a *two-ocean power*. Beijing also understands that if a war erupts in the South China Sea, and if Pakistan denies her access to Gwadar Port, then it will have serious socioeconomic implications for the country (in terms of having access to energy resources).

Pakistan awarded the contract for construction and operation to China in 2013. China Overseas Port Holding Company plans to expand Gwadar Port by constructing nine new multipurpose berths along 3.2 km of the seafront to the east of the existing berths. The shipping route from the Middle East to China via the strait is about 12,000 km long. Gwadar port will even provide alternative shipping routes to the Malacca Strait. The Port is considered a crucial link between the land-based belt and the maritime road. The investment will help strengthen Pakistan's struggling economy and also lessen its dependence on its few existing and overwhelmed ports. The CPEC will also enhance Pakistan's power generation capacity, reduce unemployment, and eliminate poverty. Although China is the main beneficiary of this mega project, one cannot deny the fact that things do not appear so simple for a lot of reasons. There are serious security concerns for China about violence from ethnic Uighurs in its predominantly Muslim north-western Xinjiang region. Political violence and schemes pushing against economic development are prevalent in that region. The economic corridor starts in Balochistan province, which has severe separatist insurgency problems. This makes that region extremely volatile. Moreover, the Baloch people (3% of its population) fear that their resources are being exploited by outsiders and that they will soon be turned into a minority group. Both the Uighur militant groups and the East Turkestan Islamic Movement (ETIM) have sought refuge in the Pakistan–Afghanistan border areas, where they have established links with other terrorist organizations. China perceives the ETIM as a persistent threat committed to targeting their nation. Now, it is important to consider whether China, in the hopes of better securing its ongoing territorial ambitions, will be able to tackle the threat of the jihadi organizations in neighboring Pakistan.

6.2.3 *India's security dilemma*

The CPEC is a reflection of escalated and enhanced bilateral cooperation at a time of rising Chinese geopolitical ambition and persistent concerns about Pakistan's security and development. India is upset with the

China–Pakistan Economic Corridor because it runs through the disputed Gilgit-Baltistan region, part of the erstwhile state of Jammu and Kashmir, which is contested by both India and Pakistan [30]. India is also worried that the Pakistan–China pipeline that runs parallel to the Karakorum highway starting from Gwadar to Kashgar in Xinjiang could turn out to be a hub for the PLA Navy [22]. The most difficult areas to control are the borders in Kashmir, where Pakistan, India, and China all have competing claims and the line of control (LOC) remains the de facto international frontier within Kashmir. Because of China's constant use of veto power to throttle India's proposal at the United Nations Security Council (UNSC), and the recent terrorist attack in Pulwama, India, in which Pakistan based Jaish-e-Muhammed (JeM) had claimed responsibility for the terror attack, the situation has worsened [8].

Both Gwadar and the Iranian Chabahar port are competing to gain access to the Central Asian Region (CAR) markets. The Chabahar port is located in the south of Sistan and Balochistan Province of Iran and is the only Iranian port with direct access to the Indian Ocean. It has historically been a trading center because of its access to the Oman Sea and the Persian Gulf. The port will be connected to the Trans-Iranian railway with the completion of the Kerman–Zahedan railway. Due to the port of Chabahar, it is easy for India to trade with Central Asian Republics, Afghanistan, and Iran. India is also providing landlocked Afghanistan greater access to the Indian market and has inaugurated an air freight corridor to boost bilateral trade. [3] Moreover, unlike Gwadar, Chabahar does not lie in a disturbing and insurgency-ridden area. Hence, strategic countries like India prefer Chabahar for easy trading and for serving personal security needs in the region. In fact, India is trying hard to consolidate its strategic interests in West Asia under its "Look West" policy. China's activity in Pakistan and Myanmar, the expansion of China's port agreements in the Indian Ocean (the so-called "string of pearls"), and heightened Chinese naval activity in the Indian Ocean are perceived threats to India's security. China is focusing on strategic encirclement or "wei qi" (known in Japan as "go"). [6] Therefore, any significant move by the Dragon made in the region would certainly bother the Elephant.

However, the security dilemma between China and India in the Indian Ocean Region (IOR) is a serious matter of concern. India is highly dependent on energy imports and has progressively sought to secure shipping lanes for the transportation of oil from Iran, Myanmar, and Sudan. Any disruptions in the Indian Ocean can lead to serious consequences for the

Indian economy. Hence, this region has become strategically significant for India. Nearly half the global seaborne trade passes through the Indian Ocean, around 40% of offshore oil production comes from the Indian Ocean, and 65% of the world's oil and 35% [1] of its gas reserves are found in the littoral states of the IOR.

6.3 Conclusion

Let her sleep, for when she wakes, she will shake the world.

— Napoleon Bonaparte

China's foreign policy is fast moving away from the old taoguang yanghui (keeping a low profile) strategy to fenfa youwei (striving for achievement) [11]. It appears that China can achieve much more with OBOR than with the South China Sea. This is because the maritime disputes in the region are difficult to resolve, at least for the foreseeable future. There are several factors that appear to be responsible for such miscalculations; for example, the failure of joint development, unnecessary complications due to China's historical claims, 9-dash-line, the UNCLOS, and vast energy resources. It appears that Beijing's policy is becoming highly assertive every day. For example, China has started growing crops like lettuce, baby cabbage, and bok choy cabbage on the sandy beaches of the Paracels. Their idea is to help and support the community with agriculture. However, the long-term goal is to sustain an export market that will further strengthen their claim to sovereignty on the island.

Former President Hu Jintao defined the objective of China's foreign policy as to "jointly construct a harmonious world," and invoked the cultural idea of "all under heaven," or Tianxia [15]. If his statement is true, the question remains whether China will continue to undertake aggressive actions in the SCS to advance its territorial claims and satisfy its rapidly increasing energy demands. However, to what extent China will continue to pursue an assertive policy in the South China Sea depends on time, as Beijing has neither identified nor denied the South China Sea issue as one of its core interests. Besides, core interests are often non-negotiable in nature (like the sovereignty of Tibet). As Michael Swain comments: China will "never waiver, compromise, or yield," and "stand firm, be clear, have the courage to fight and never surrender." [10] Such strategic ambiguity has only resulted in greater dilemmas in the regional and global sphere.

China cannot always use its history to justify its claims and get support from her neighbors. Besides, the concept of historical rights has not been fully developed in international law, and it is a daunting challenge for China and other stakeholders in the region.

On the contrary, although OBOR is primarily an economic initiative, it has significant political and strategic dimensions that cannot be overlooked. Beijing believes that OBOR will help them in winning the confidence of its neighbors and also strengthen its influence on the global economic and political stage. It could eventually become a future policy choice for China. As scholars of international relations, we should not forget that our *future lies together*. Therefore, it is essential that we gain "a better understanding and recognition of the contents, objectives, and tasks of the Belt and Road." [24] It is very difficult to predict the promise vs. the reality of these Chinese economic initiatives. China has often overpromised lofty ambitions for future investment projects, but in reality, it has failed to deliver. Perhaps it is only speculative at this stage since some of these BRI projects have yet to fully materialize. Overall, the idea is to take small steps forward, and gradually cross the river, achieving more sustainable options along the way — similar to Deng Xiaoping's remarks during the economic reforms of the 1980s, "crossing the river by feeling the stones." [29]

As China's territorial and jurisdictional claims in the South China Sea are getting highly contentious, the question stands whether China should continue to pursue an assertive position in the South China Sea or learn to adjust its policy. In 2020, the situation almost got out of control, and scholars even predicted the dangers of war in the South China Sea region. China has performed several naval exercises and also ramped up its military industries amid the COVID-19 pandemic. Such aggressive behavior is raising tensions amongst its neighbors and creating scenarios for regional backlash. If this continues, then it might be harmful to China and further undermine her ideas of promoting cooperation and development via the OBOR strategy. Hence, the dragon needs to identify its priorities and understand what should come first: the OBOR, or upholding China's claims in the South China Sea.

To conclude, Silk Road commerce should aim to bring peaceful resolutions to hostile communities, enhance effective diplomatic contracts, and, finally, become the symbol for modern international commerce. Beijing's reemergence and reintegration — mainly in the form of Silk Road economic dynamism — will depend on several factors, including how well BRI nations are willing to negotiate with each other. Most are still in the planning stages. We also need to wait and see how many initiatives will actually be implemented. OBOR could be the driving factor in China's emergence from a regional hegemon to global power. Only time will tell if China is heading in the right direction and if OBOR will be the road to the future or if it will turn into Donald Trumps' "covfefe." [8]

References

1. Arabinda, K. A. (2006). India and Southeast Asia in the age of terror: building partnerships for peace. *Contemporary Southeast Asia*, *28*(2): 297–321.
2. Shepherd, C., Wen, P., & Perry, M. (2017). China expresses concern over reported Duterte South China Sea comments. *The Star*. https://www.thestar.com.my/news/world/2017/04/07/china-expresses-concern-over-reported-duterte-south-china-sea-comments.
3. Chawla, M. I. (2017). One belt one road summit 2017 and its implications for CPEC: An overview. *Research Journal of South Asian Studies*, *32*(2): 277–284.
4. Chin, T. (2013). The invention of the silk road, 1877. *Critical Inquiry*, *40*(1): 194–219. https://doi.org/10.1086/673232.
5. Nie, W. (2016). Xi Jinping's foreign policy dilemma: One belt, one road or the South China Sea? *Contemporary Southeast Asia*, *38*(3): 422–444.
6. Roy, N. (2016). *The South China Sea disputes: Past, present and future*. Rowman & Littlefield. pp. 78–79.
7. Roy, N. (2017). The dragon's charm diplomacy in the South China Sea. *Journal of Asian Affairs*, 30: 1–2, June–December, pp. 15–28.
8. Roy, N. (2019). China-Pakistan economic corridor — Is it the road to the future? *Asian Affairs*, *50*(2): 268–282, DOI: 10.1080/03068374.2019.1614767.
9. Storey, I. (2006). China's "Malacca Dilemma." *China Brief*, *6*(8), https://jamestown.org/program/chinas-malacca-dilemma/.
10. Swaine, M. D. (2011). China's assertive behavior part one: On "Core Interests." *China Leadership Monitor, 34*(7).
11. Yan, X. (2014). From keeping a low profile to striving for achievement. *Chinese Journal of International Politics*, *7*(2): 153–184.
12. Friedman, G. (2019). *The World Explained in Maps*. Mauldin Economics. https://mauldineconomics.com/download/the-world-explained-in-maps-free-e-book.
13. Roberts, H. (2018). The Rational Behind the China-Pakistan Economic Corridor: The View from Beijing, in David Lane and Guichang Zhu (Eds.) *Changing Regional Alliances for China and the West*. Lexington Books.

14. Segal, G. & Yang, R. (Eds.) (1996). *Chinese Economic Reform: The Impact on Security*. London: Routledge, p. 142.
15. Acharya, A. (2011). Can Asia Step Up to 21st Century Leadership? *Yale Global*. http://yaleglobal.yale.edu/content/can-asia-step-21st-century-leadership.
16. Associated Press. (2017). Quotes from leaders at China's New Silk Road meeting. *Fox*. https://www.foxbusiness.com/markets/quotes-from-leaders-at-chinas-new-silk-road-meeting.
17. Duhalde, M., Arranz, A., & Hernandez, M. (2018). The Five Main Projects of the Belt and Road Initiative. *SCMP*. http://multimedia.scmp.com/news/china/article/One-Belt-One-Road/index.html.
18. Georg, W. (2018). The Future of Tourism on the New Silk Route. *China Outbound Tourism Research Institute*. https://china-outbound.com/wp-content/uploads/2018/04/silkroad2018Arlt.pdf.
19. Herberg, M. E. (2011). *Natural Gas in Asia: History and Prospects*. The National Bureau of Asian Research, Pacific Energy Summit.
20. HKTDC. (2018). The Belt and Road Initiative. *Hong Kong Trade Development Council*. http://china-trade-research.hktdc.com/business-news/article/The-Belt-and-Road-Initiative/The-Belt-and-Road-Initiative-Country-Profiles/obor/en/1/1X000000/1X0A36I0.htm.
21. Husain, K. (2017). Exclusive: CPEC master plan revealed. *Dawn*. https://www.dawn.com/news/1333101.
22. Kulshrestha, S. (n.d.). A Tale of Two Ports: Gwadar versus Chabahar. *New Westminster College, Canada*. http://worldnewsreport.in/a-tale-of-two-ports-gwadar-versus-chabahar/. Retrieved on April, 2020.
23. Markey, D. & West, J. (2016). Behind China's Gambit in Pakistan. *CFR*. https://www.cfr.org/expert-brief/behind-chinas-gambit-pakistan.
24. Ministry of Foreign Affairs (2015). *Vision and Actions on Jointly Building Silk Road Economic Belt and 21st-Century Maritime Silk Road*. Issued by the National Development and Reform Commission, Ministry of Foreign Affairs, and Ministry of Commerce of the People's Republic of China. http://en.ndrc.gov.cn/newsrelease/201503/t20150330_669367.html.
25. National Bureau of Asian Research. (2011). *Unlocking the Potential of Natural Gas in the Asia-Pacific*. Pacific Energy Summit. http://www.nbr.org/downloads/pdfs/ETA/PES2011_summitreport.pdf.
26. Rafiq, A. (2017). The China-Pakistan Economic Corridor: Barriers and Impact. *U.S. Institute of Peace*. https://www.usip.org/publications/2017/10/china-pakistan-economic-corridor.
27. Stanslas, P. (2010). *The Spratly Dilemma: External powers and Dispute Resolution Mechanisms*, Biuletyn: Opinie.
28. Staff. (2016). Belt and Road: China's Grand Gambit. *HSBC*. https://www.weekinchina.com/zine/focus-editions/belt-and-road/.

29. Staff. (2016). What is Belt and Road? *HSBC*. https://www.weekinchina.com/?p=32823.
30. The Economist. (2012). Indian, Pakistani and Chinese border disputes: Fantasy Frontiers. *The Economist*. https://www.economist.com/graphic-detail/2012/02/08/fantasy-frontiers.
31. U.S. Energy Information Administration. (2012). "China: Country Analysis Brief." *EIA*. http://www.eia.gov/countries/analysisbriefs/China/china.pdf.
32. Xinhua. (2013). Making "Chinese dream" a reality. *China Daily*. http://www.chinadaily.com.cn/china/2013-12/08/content_17160305.htm.

https://doi.org/10.1142/9781786349286_0007

Chapter 7

Conclusion: Will Saber-rattling Continue in the South China Sea?

Nalanda Roy and Daniel Katz

7.1 South China Sea — A Current Potential Flashpoint

The Dutch legal scholar Hugo Grotius argued in the *Mare Liberum* [1] that the ocean's bounty is inexhaustible, as limitless as the air; thus, it "cannot become a possession of anyone." However, the South China Sea (SCS) remains a highly volatile environment because of its potential energy resources and importance as a vital sea lane for communication. It has become apparent that the claimant states are willing to employ military force to assert control over such resources. In fact, the SCS region and the coastal passage from Malaysia to Russia has become an area of vital geoeconomic interest to all. Territorial disputes both in the South and East China Seas, the growth of "energy nationalism," as well as military build-ups by China, Japan, and other external powers like the United States have created a highly unstable environment.

Although China and the Association of Southeast Asian Nations (ASEAN) have made some progress over a code of conduct (COC) to reduce tensions in the SCS, Beijing has shown no sign of relenting in its construction of military facilities and land reclamation strategies in the region. President Xi Jinping had mentioned that China will directly consult with countries involved in disputes based on historical facts and continue to seek resolution of the same through peaceful negotiations and consultations in accordance with international laws. [4] Beijing has established fuel and ammunition depots, radar facilities, and runways on Fiery Cross Reef, Subi Reef, and Mischief Reef. Additionally, China began oil exploration in Vietnam's Exclusive Economic Zone (EEZ) and collided with Philippine as well as Vietnamese fishing boats. In fact, the COC appears more tenuous by the day. Tensions are escalating in the Taiwan Strait due to Beijing's friction with the U.S. In this situation, it appears that the best way forward for China is to broker an agreement with ASEAN on the COC so that the PRC can direct its attention to the role of the U.S. in the SCS. China apparently wants to conclude drafting the COC before the Philippines' role as country coordinator for ASEAN-China Dialogue Relations expires in 2021 because, unlike his predecessor, President Rodrigo Duterte might adopt a more conciliatory approach towards Beijing (perhaps with the prospect of receiving economic aid from China).

In 2016, at the behest of the Philippines, an international arbitration panel in The Hague, Netherlands, rejected China's 9-dash line claim and asserted that it has no basis in international law per the U.N. Convention on the Law of the Sea (UNCLOS). Since that time, China has dissented and ignored the ruling. However, China believes that it can use the code to extricate itself from the ruling; both China and the Philippines are trying to resolve their dispute peacefully and expeditiously. Beijing has three basic demands regarding the COC. First, it should not be covered by the UNCLOS treaty; next, if any foreign joint military exercises occur in the region, they must have the prior consent of all parties and reach an agreement; and finally, resource development should not be conducted with countries outside the region. Such moves indicate that it is essential to opt for a crisis management system in the contested waters.

Going forward, countries should pay particular attention to the SCS as it will become a potential flashpoint in international security. China will likely adopt a bolder stance and act more aggressively in the future. There will be intensifying security competition, thereby raising the probability of direct and dangerous conflicts. In the East China Sea, both Japan and China are increasing their military presence. Additionally, the growing rift between Japan and South Korea will fracture regional political opposition. In the Spratly Islands, China is establishing more military outposts, occupying the Scarborough shoal with unmanned drones, and further militarizing its current outposts in the Paracels and Spratlys. Beijing has also approved two new administrative centers in the SCS. In April 2020, both the Paracel and Spratly Islands were put under Chinese control. It was even decided that Sansha city will now control both the districts. Such activities will give Beijing access to islands far away from the mainland, and also safeguard its national sovereignty.

China could become increasingly confrontational in several territorial disputes and spark tension among its neighbors in the regional maritime domain. However, China might be reluctant to alter its current behavior as it continues to attempt to establish de facto control over the SCS via legal, economic, military, and even diplomatic measures. It is possible that China might conduct increased joint naval exercises with Russia in the belief that the U.S. would not challenge both rivals simultaneously. In addition, China perceives that America's military advantage is waning. China increasingly relies upon anti-access area-denial (A2AD) capabilities to create asymmetric advantages for its forces, which imperils historic U.S. warfighting tactics. The U.S. has to devise ways to extend its sphere of influence in the region in order to prevent China from dominating access to what has been termed the first island chain. The U.S. might seek to leverage its alliances and partnerships with other Southeast Asian countries to provide more political support and greater military access in the region. For example, the U.S. has decided to sail its naval vessels through the Taiwan Strait regularly as part of freedom of navigation operations (FONOPs) and even sought to expand Taiwan's international space. Taiwan's Defense Ministry even stated that "a Taiwan-U.S. military exchange and cooperation plan will not only help to consolidate and strengthen the security partnership between the two sides and also ensure peace and stability in the region." [2]

7.2 Geopolitical Tools in the South China Sea

7.2.1 *COVID-19 and the South China Sea*

The novel coronavirus that emerged in the city of Wuhan, China, in late 2019 has spread to more than 200 countries and territories and has since become a large-scale COVID-19 epidemic. As of April 2020, over 3 million COVID-19 cases have been documented, with over 250,000 deaths across the globe. It appears that the pandemic has complicated both the geopolitical and the geoeconomic situation in the region. For example, there is pressure to invite Taiwan to participate in the World Health Organization (WHO) because the exclusion of Taiwan during the pandemic will put both the Taiwanese and the world at greater risk. Infectious diseases know no borders, and hence involving Taiwan will lead to the promotion of multilateral cooperation in the region. Pandemics and politics do not mix, however, and Beijing has continued to press the WHO to exclude Taiwan from joining the WHO. China also used its influence campaigns and economic incentives to boost its preferred candidate Han Kuo-yu in Taiwan's 2020 presidential election. However, the re-election of President Tsai Ing-wen in 2019 signaled a political setback for China. After coming to power, Tsai has called for a peaceful resolution of the SCS disputes and advocated for freedom of navigation in the SCS, even announcing that Taiwan will continue to strengthen its ties with Japan.

From the Chinese perspective, the COVID-19 pandemic has impaired the U.S. Navy's warship deployment capability in the Asia-Pacific region. Similar to the period following the 2008 global financial crisis, China perceives American weakness and therefore uses it as an opening for the opportunistic seizing of military and soft power advantage over the U.S. While China is preparing to increase operations in the SCS, the U.S. military has had to address COVID-19 outbreaks on its Pacific aircraft carriers as well as other vessels. China has performed a large-scale naval exercise and ramped up its military industries in Wuhan, the epicenter of the pandemic. Such an aggressive approach by China amid COVID-19 will only raise tensions amongst its neighbors and could create a regional backlash. For example, the SCS exercise transpired immediately after the U.S. aircraft carrier USS Theodore Roosevelt passed through the region. Later, the ship was docked in Guam where the outbreak of COVID-19 occurred. The USS Ronald Reagan aircraft carrier in the Pacific also dealt with an outbreak of COVID-19, and was initially docked in Yokosuka, Japan, to deal with the pandemic. However, the recent involvement of the USS Barry, a guided-missile destroyer near the Paracels, and the arms cruiser USS Bunker Hill aircraft carrier in the disputed islands has sparked fresh disturbances in the SCS. The U.S. navy is highlighting such operations in China's near abroad, and the U.S. PACOM commander Phil Davidson said "Preserving a free and open Indo-Pacific is a core interest of the United States." [3] Beijing has stated that these actions are not only provocative but have also violated international law and China's sovereignty.

If the U.S. decides to reduce its regional naval presence due to the pandemic, the PLA (People's Liberation Army) might take advantage of the situation due to the perception of a strategic vacuum. Beijing could opportunistically attempt to utilize the global pandemic to gain geopolitical influence in the region. China's aggressive behavior is not only antagonizing its Indo-Pacific neighbors but also risks alienating ASEAN. Beijing's continued presence in Indonesia's EEZ is sending a negative signal to the Indonesian government and is considered a challenge to Indonesia's territorial sovereignty. In early April 2020, China rammed and sank a Vietnamese fishing boat in the vicinity of the Paracel Islands. The incident occurred in waters controlled by China but claimed by Vietnam. Such provocations act as constant triggers and worsen the peace and stability in the region.

7.2.2 *Belt and Road Initiative (BRI) and the South China Sea*

The Belt and Road Initiative (BRI) is an ambitious vision for China that emphasizes opening up and cooperation among the participating countries. Such joint initiatives can increase China's access to foreign markets and uphold the global free trade regime. The Initiative is pluralistic and is also based on an open process of cooperation, which makes it highly flexible. The question is whether BRI can act as a "soft" balancing strategy in the SCS and be a "game-changer" both in the regional sphere and on the global stage. The BRI can significantly alter Asia's emerging international order, and even accelerate contests and forge cooperation in the region. To date, however, the track record of BRI has been less than promised and places partner countries at risk of entering debt traps and resultant defaults. Amid the COVID-19 outbreak, BRI partner countries may even confront significant challenges in meeting debt obligations due to reduced economic activity. The BRI spirit embraces a multipolar world, economic globalization, geoeconomic connections, technological advancement, and cultural diversity; however, the biggest question is whether countries have a choice in deciding whether or not to join such initiatives. It is unknown whether China will seek to leverage the BRI into furthering its hegemonic ambitions in the region. Only time will tell if the BRI is merely tactical and marked with opportunism or if it is a way for win–win cooperation towards peace and prosperity in the SCS.

7.3 Final Thoughts

Disputes among claimant countries in the South China Sea have been continuing for decades. Previous attempts to mitigate tensions in this vital maritime domain have largely failed. Although other countries have attempted to assert their rights, China is particularly notable for its enlargement of existing features and construction efforts on previously uninhabited islands. While China maintains that its activities are entirely peaceful, the sum of its behavior has been to militarize the SCS. U.S. aircraft and naval vessels have been met with hostile warnings by China asserting its rightful ownership of the islands as well as control over surrounding waters and airspace.

The key contemporary challenge is how to resolve the seeming impasse of SCS dynamics. To date, China has declined to yield from its expansive claims over the entirety of the SCS. Its preference for bilateral negotiations with claimant states rather than multilateral approaches via ASEAN favors Chinese interests. It is essential that Southeast Asian countries bordering the SCS as well as the U.S. uphold the principle of freedom of navigation through these waters, which are vital to global commerce and security. In order to alter Chinese behavior, it will, therefore, be necessary to shape the calculus of the PRC vis-à-vis the SCS.

The first component of a more successful path forward is to emphasize the downside of continued Chinese noncompliance. Military deterrence — the "stick" of the "carrot and stick" approach — is a key aspect of a two-pronged solution. The U.S. military can play a major supporting role in such efforts in collaboration with like-minded countries, especially through a high operational tempo of FONOPs. Along these lines, the 2018 National Defense Strategy of the U.S. Department of Defense (DOD) authored under the leadership of former Secretary of Defense James Mattis emphasized the U.S. intention to be "strategically predictable, but operationally unpredictable." As of mid-2020 the U.S. military is increasingly operationalizing this strategy through a wide variety of air and sea deployments. Nonetheless, there is a risk that unsafe military encounters could result in the loss of life, which no country desires. Bolstering existing conflict-avoidance mechanisms such as CUES might ameliorate the potential for unintentional escalation. Since China extensively employs its coast guard and maritime militia throughout its territorial waters and the SCS, regional countries would do well to incorporate these forces in addition to conventional naval vessels into any future maritime agreements.

In addition, the use of gray-zone tactics by China below the traditional threshold of conflict requires creative thinking to defuse tensions.

Another component of a strategy to defuse tensions in the SCS relies upon finding mutually beneficial solutions — the "carrot." Unrestricted commerce in the SCS benefits all countries that ply its waters. The COC has the potential to ensure that all countries can safely navigate the SCS without fear of reprisal. However, the issues of enforcement mechanisms and the extent to which the COC will be legally binding loom large. There are ample energy and marine resources in the SCS for all claimant countries. It is therefore in everyone's best interest to cooperate. China is the main trading partner for countries throughout Asia as well as many Western countries. Since Chinese exports depend upon maritime transit through the SCS, it is counterproductive for China to impede unrestricted access to these waters. While nationalism is a potent factor within China, economic growth is vital to the continued survival of the Chinese Communist Party (CCP). It is in Beijing's best interests to curtail its nationalist impulses in the service of economic objectives.

The U.S. has functioned as the de facto hegemon in the Indo-Pacific region since the end of World War II. Significant military modernization and profound economic growth have catapulted China to near-peer status with the U.S. Despite its denials, China does aspire to displace the U.S. as the regional hegemon. No country in Southeast Asia desires to choose between allegiance to China or the U.S. The more belligerent China behaves vis-à-vis its neighbors, the greater the probability of Southeast Asian balancing behavior towards the U.S. A stable equilibrium would better serve all countries in the region and reduce the risk of conflict.

The SCS issue has increasingly drawn the attention of non-claimant states such as Australia, France, India, Indonesia, Japan, and the UK. It is conceivable that multiple countries could partner in maritime exercises to deter expansionist Chinese behavior. Nations which seek to promote a positive vision of unrestricted freedom of navigation within the SCS must move from a strategy of limited deterrence to one of coercive diplomacy. It is too late to adopt pure deterrence since China has been engaged in widespread island reclamation activity and militarization of the SCS for numerous years. A coercive diplomacy approach would aim to reverse Chinese behavior through the threat or actual use of limited force.

It is increasingly likely that the security competition in the SCS will instigate a crisis should escalation dynamics continue unabated. Sooner or later, Southeast Asian countries might demand that Beijing cease its ongoing maritime harassment. Without a doubt, 2020 will be challenging not only for the U.S. and China but also for countries in the region that are caught in the crossfire. We can only hope that China will do its best to maintain the South China Sea as a zone of peace, freedom, friendship, and cooperation (ZoPFFC). In order to reverse the trend towards conflict, countries within the ASEAN must be proactive and engage in multinational efforts.

References

1. Grotuis, H. (1916). *The Freedom of the Seas; Or, The Right which Belongs to the Dutch to Take Part in the East Indian Trade.* Oxford University Press.
2. Shepherd, C., Wen, P., & Perry, M. (2017). China expresses concern over reported Duterte South China Sea comments. *U.S. News*. https://www.usnews.com/news/world/articles/2017-04-07/china-expresses-concern-over-reported-duterte-south-china-sea-comments.
3. Davidson, P. S. (2019). Statement of Admiral Phillip S. Davidson, U.S. Navy Commander, U.S. Indo-Pacific Command Before the Senate Armed Forces Committee on U.S. Indo-Pacific Command Posture. Senate Armed Forces Committee. https://www.armed-services.senate.gov/imo/media/doc/Davidson_02-12-19.pdf.
4. Ministry of Foreign Affairs of the People's Republic of China. (2014). Position Paper of the Government of the People's Republic of China on the Matter of Jurisdiction in the South China Sea Arbitration Initiated by the Republic of the Philippines. Published for the South China Sea Arbitration. https://america.cgtn.com/2016/07/11/chinas-position-paper-on-the-south-china-sea-arbitration.

https://doi.org/10.1142/9781786349286_bmatter

Index

CPSIA information can be obtained
at www.ICGtesting.com
Printed in the USA
LVHW081759081220
673628LV00001B/18

9 781786 349279